Contemporary Social Issues

Contemporary Social Issues

Authentic Readings for the ESL Learner

Sarabel Kass Cohen

Ann Arbor

THE UNIVERSITY OF MICHIGAN PRESS

Acknowledgments

I would like to express my appreciation to Dr. Patricia Byrd, professor in the Applied Linguistics/ESL Department at Georgia State University, for her sincere interest in the writing of this book. She took time from her busy schedule to read the manuscript and offered valuable suggestions. Dr. Byrd has been an inspiration to me as well as to her many graduate students at Georgia State.

I would also like to thank Professor Linda Gajdusek, Director of the English Language Center at Northeastern University, who read the incomplete manuscript and made helpful comments and suggestions.

Further thanks go to Professor Sharon Cavusgil, AL/ESL Department at Georgia State, who wrote the first of the two summaries of the excerpt from Dr. William Bennett's book, *Our Children & Our Country.*

I am grateful to Seth Cohen, attorney, for his summary of the Family and Medical Leave Act.

Many thanks to my always interesting students without whom I could not have written this book.

And, of course, a very special thank you to my husband, Gilbert, and our children, Kass, Seth, and Patricia Kinney, for their interest and encouragement.

Grateful acknowledgment is given to the following publishers for use of copyrighted material:

The New York Times Company for "In Crowded Japan, a Bonus for Babies Angers Women" by Steven R. Weisman, *New York Times,* February 17, 1991, copyright © 1991 by The New York Times Company; "China, with Ever More to Feed, Pushes Anew for Small Families" by Sheryl WuDunn, *New York Times,* June 16, 1991, copyright © 1991 by The New York Times Company; "The Decay of Families Is Global, Study Says" and "Compare and Contrast; Family Ties" (graphic) by Tamar Lewin, *New York Times,* May 30, 1995, copyright © 1995 by The New York Times Company; and for "Healthy Korean Economy Draws Immigrants Home" by Pam Belluck, *New York Times*, August 22, 1995, copyright © 1995 by The New York Times Company. Reprinted by permission.

Wichita Eagle for "It May Not Be Too Late for the World to Come to Grips with Overpopulation," by Myrne Roe. Reprinted by permission.

World Book, Inc., for excerpts from "The 1990 Census: An American Self-Portrait," by Karin C. Rosenberg. From *The 1992 World Book Year Book.* Copyright © 1992 World Book, Inc. By permission of the publisher.

AJC Newsearch for "In 2050 America Will Be . . ." originally published as "Census Bureau Paints America's Future," including graph, by Carrie Teegardin, *Atlanta Journal and Constitution*; and for "A Sharp, Beribboned Message to Abusive Husbands" by Joe Murray, *Atlanta Journal and Constitution*. Reprinted by permission.

Time Inc., for excerpt from "Teach Your Children Well" by Paul Gray, *Time,* Fall 1993. Copyright © 1993 Time Inc. Reprinted by permission.

Parade Publications for "What Is a Family?" by Bernard Gavzer, *Parade*, November 22, 1992, copyright © 1992. Reprinted with permission from Parade and the author.

Peachtree Publishers, LTD to reprint chapter 5 of *Mothers Are Always Special* by Celestine Sibley. Copyright © 1970, 1985 Celestine Sibley. Reprinted by permission.

Allyn & Bacon for "The Modern Family," excerpted from *Sociology Brief Edition–1992* by Beth B. Hess, Elizabeth W. Markson & Peter J. Stein. Copyright © 1992. All rights reserved. Reprinted/adapted by permission of Allyn & Bacon.

The Washington Post Writers Group for "Family Secrets" by Ellen Goodman, copyright © 1985, The Boston Globe Newspaper Co./Washington Post Writers Group; and for "Home Is the Key to Our Kids' Success in School" by William Raspberry, copyright © 1992, Washington Post Writers Group. Reprinted with permission.

Doubleday for "Chen Ning Yang," excerpted from *Bill Moyers: A World of Ideas* by Bill Moyers. Copyright © 1989 by Public Affairs Television, Inc. Used by permission of Doubleday, a division of Bantam Doubleday Dell Publishing Group, Inc.

San Jose Mercury News for "Parents, Get Serious about Raising Your Kids" by Joanne Jacobs, *San Jose Mercury News,* copyright © 1995, San Jose Mercury News. All rights reserved. Reproduced with permission.

Simon & Schuster for excerpt from *Our Children & Our Country* by William J. Bennett. Copyright © 1988 by Simon & Schuster, Inc. Reprinted with the permission of Simon & Schuster.

Scientific American, Inc., for excerpt from *Indochinese Refugee Families and Academic Achievement* by Nathan Caplan, Marcella H. Choy, and John K. Whitmore, *Scientific American*, February 1992. Copyright © 1992 by Scientific American, Inc. All rights reserved. Reprinted with permission.

HarperCollins for summary of SQR3 Learning Method from *Effective Study*, 4th ed., by Francis Robinson. Copyright 1941, 1946 by Harper & Row, Publishers, Inc. Copyright © 1961, 1970 by Francis P. Robinson. Reprinted by permission of HarperCollins Publishers, Inc.

Every effort has been made to trace the ownership of all copyrighted material in this book and to obtain permission for its use.

Introduction

This reading text was designed for preacademic English as a second language (ESL) students at the high-intermediate level. The purpose of the text is to help ESL students become better readers by furnishing them with authentic reading materials accompanied by exercises that provide practice in the development of various reading and language skills—skills that students can transfer to other reading materials when they begin their academic studies.

Reading Selections

The reading selections deal with interesting contemporary issues and are arranged thematically.

Population Control	3 chapters
The Census; Immigration	3 chapters
Family	5 chapters
Education	5 chapters

The selections come from a variety of sources: newspapers; magazines; an encyclopedia; a college textbook; and books of essays, true stories, transcribed conversations, and speeches. Among the writers are two Pulitzer Prize winners, Ellen Goodman and William Raspberry; award-winning journalist and columnist Celestine Sibley; and former U.S. Secretary of Education, William J. Bennett.

The Exercises and Activities

Prereading Activities

The *prereading questions* give students an idea of what they are about to read and help to activate any prior knowledge they might have about the subject.

The *skimming* exercises also give students a general idea of what a reading is about, and they offer practice in rapid reading, a skill needed by students in degree programs that require massive amounts of reading.

Scanning Exercises

The *scanning* exercises provide practice in reading rapidly in order to find specific information, an important skill for reading in academic settings.

Reading Comprehension Exercises

The *reading comprehension* exercises help students recognize main ideas, focus on important details, and make necessary inferences; they include questions and discussion about the selections, true/false statements, and multiple choice items.

Study Reading

One technique used in mastering textbook material is the SQ3R method. An excerpt from a sociology textbook gives students the opportunity to practice this technique.

Paraphrasing and Summarizing

Several chapters in this text stress *paraphrasing* and *summarizing,* skills that are essential for academic success. Students learn to clarify difficult sentences and to summarize information from written material. The latter skill is of great help in taking examinations.

Reading Critically

Critical reading is an essential skill for academic study. Students are given questions that guide them in making judgments about what they have read: the author's purpose, point of view, credibility, reliability of sources, and so forth.

Responding to the Readings

Students are given the opportunity to voice their opinions—in writing or orally—about what they have read. They may wish to read their written responses to their classmates.

Vocabulary Study

Guessing-from-Context Exercises

The numerous *guessing-from-context* exercises in this text give students practice in guessing the meanings of words from context. Students become less dependent on their dictionaries, thereby enabling them to read with more speed.

Glossaries

Some of the chapters in this text contain *glossaries,* which are helpful to students as they read.

Vocabulary Review

At the end of each unit, there is a review of the new vocabulary studied in that unit.

Opportunities to Write

This text provides students with opportunities to *write.*

Answers to discussion questions

Comparison and contrast

Responding to the reading selections

Paraphrasing and summarizing

Supplementary Readings

The two supplementary readings continue with the themes of Immigration (Unit 2) and Family (Unit 3). Each selection is followed by a glossary and a few questions to test reading comprehension.

For the Teacher

I think that the instructions throughout the text are sufficiently explicit to be helpful to students and teachers alike. I would like to add a few suggestions for the teacher.

— The *prereading questions* and the *skimming exercises* are *in-class* activities. The prereading questions give students an idea of what they are about to read, help to activate any prior knowledge they might have about the subject, and generate interesting discussion. The skimming exercises also give students a general idea of what a reading selection is about, and they offer practice in rapid reading.

— I recommend that the *first reading* of a selection be done *in class.* The teacher might read aloud an entire short selection or part of a longer one. In the latter case, the students finish reading silently. (No dictionaries should be allowed during this reading.)

— The *guessing-from-context* exercises (vocabulary study) can be done *in class* immediately after the first reading. Students work in pairs or groups, the teacher offering help when needed. (When this exercise is done at home, students are tempted to use their dictionaries instead of trying to guess the meanings of unfamiliar words.)

— If the *reading comprehension* exercises are assigned as homework, the answers to the questions should be discussed at the next class meeting.

— I recommend that the *critical reading* exercises be done *in class,* the teacher leading and directing the discussion.

— Finally, the chapters in the text should be presented in sequence.

Note: The deleted paragraph on page 103 can be found on page 112.

Contents

1. In Crowded Japan, a Bonus for Babies Angers Women

(by Steven R. Weisman, New York Times*)*

Preparing to Read

Skimming

Skimming is reading hurriedly in order to get the general idea of what a reading selection is about. Skim the following newspaper article from the *New York Times*. Look at the *title* and read the *first two* or *three paragraphs*. Then quickly run your eyes over the remainder of the article. *Do not read every word; do not read every sentence.* This should take only a matter of minutes.

In your own words, what is the *main idea* of the article? (Hint: The title can often help you recognize the main idea of a reading.)

_____

_____

Skimming is an important reading skill. *Why?*

BEFORE YOU READ THE ARTICLE THROUGH, THINK ABOUT THE ANSWERS TO THE FOLLOWING QUESTIONS.

— Do you think that the government has the right to interfere with a woman's choice to have or not to have children? Why or why not?

— Are women in your country showing dissatisfaction with the traditional role of homemaker? Do many women work outside the home?

Suggestions for Reading

In order to thoroughly understand a reading selection, you may have to read it *more than once—perhaps several times.*

— After skimming the selection, read it through without looking up any unfamiliar words.

— Do the vocabulary exercise (guessing meaning from context) that accompanies the reading.

— Read the selection again, carefully. If the chapter has a glossary (a list of the difficult words in a text and their definitions) refer to it when necessary.

— Use your dictionary as a last resort.

In Crowded Japan, a Bonus For Babies Angers Women

By STEVEN R. WEISMAN
Special to The New York Times

1 TOKYO, Feb. 16—With its crowded roads, overstuffed commuter trains and cramped housing, Japan would hardly seem to be in need of more people. So when the Government recently started telling the Japanese to bear more children, many people, especially women, became incensed.

2 The focus of their irritation was a soon-to-be-offered "reward" of 5,000 yen, or $38, a month for each child of pre-school age, and twice as much for a third child, the centerpiece of a spreading campaign to combat a birth rate that has plummeted to its lowest level in history.

'Trying to Be Equal'

3 The baby bonuses were inspired by officials concerned that at the current rate, Japan's population will decline after the turn of the century, causing labor shortages, sluggish economic growth and higher tax burdens to support social services for the elderly.

4 Countering their view are feminists and family-planning experts who find it absurd to be concerned about underpopulation. "I don't understand why the Government is worried," said Shizue Kato, the 93-year-old head of the Japan Family Planning Association.

5 She added: "In my view, we should tell the women of Japan they are wonderful women, they have reduced the birth rate so rapidly. After all, they are only trying to be equal with the men of this country."

6 Indeed, women generally see the Government's population drive as a test of their freedom. Typical is Rie Fujinishi, a 29-year-old homemaker who struggles full time with housework and the care of a 3-year-old son, and is envious of her friends who work, go out to lunch or vacation in Hawaii.

7 "I really have to laugh," Mrs. Fujinishi said of the new baby bonuses. "The Government's thinking is so simplistic. They figure if they pay a little money, the mother will have another baby, just like a machine. I won't be influenced by it. My freedom is more important than 5,000 yen."

The Long Work Day

8 Many experts are troubled by the reasons cited by Japanese women who decide to postpone marriage or have only one or two children, if they have any at all. Many Japanese women say they are in effect revolting against a system stacked against them.

9 They complain about the high cost of education, the lack of day care, the scarcity of decent or affordable housing and the physical and emotional burdens of raising children when their husbands work from early morning until they stagger home on the last subway train toward midnight.

10 "It's not a militant thing, but we're seeing a kind of 'women's revenge' in this country," said Shigemi Kono, director general of the Institute of Population Problems at the Health and Welfare Ministry. "Women are showing their disenchantment with what marriage in Japan has become."

11 Declining birth rates are a feature of all modern industrial societies, including other rapidly developing nations in Asia where work opportunities are opening up for women and social security systems are taking the place of children caring for their aging parents.

12 But no other country in the world has experienced the steady and rapid drop in birth rates that Japan has seen over the last two decades. In 1989, the fertility rate, or the average number of children a woman is expected to bear, fell to 1.57, and Mr. Kono said it is expected to drop still further.

Late Marriages

13 The causes of the drop in the birth rate, not to mention the debate and concerns it has provoked, offer a lesson in how increasing wealth has not brought increasing happiness among the Japanese.

14 Today two-thirds of the men and a third of the women do not marry until their 30's. Only in Sweden do people marry later, but unlike Sweden and other places, Japan is a country where unmarried couples almost never live together.

15 Women say they are more interested in careers, education and the attractions of a single lifestyle. They complain about living in tiny apartments, about the drudgery of marriage to demanding husbands who do not help at home, and about the near impossibility of mixing work and motherhood.

16 "Sometimes I admit I'm very lonely," said Kay Suzuki, a 32-year-old unmarried office worker. "But I just can't imagine quitting my job. My boyfriend finally gave up trying to get me to marry him. He was a typical Japanese man. He didn't want a partner, he wanted me to be his mother."

17 Every expert has an opinion, it seems, about why the trend is occurring. One scholar recently suggested that sports, video games and other diversions were robbing men of their libido. Others bemoan the absence of places for men and women to meet and go off together.

A Throne Goes Begging?

18 Humorists note that even so eligible a bachelor as Crown Prince Naruhito, the 31-year-old son of the Emperor of Japan, is having trouble finding a bride—and future empress—because few women of high social standing are willing to surrender their freedom to the imperial family.*

19 The plummeting birth rate is cited darkly by ultranationalists, who speak of sapping Japan's "ethnic vitality." One publication warned in all seriousness last year that at the current rate, Japan's population would decline to 45,000 by the year 3000. The population now is more than 123 million.

20 The Government warns more persuasively of a shrinking tax base and skyrocketing demands for government services, especially for the elderly. But officials fear that promoting births would remind people of the coercive 1930's campaign to "breed and multiply" for the good of the Japanese empire.

21 "It's a difficult problem that threatens the future of our social welfare system," said Saburo Toida, chairman of a Parliamentary committee on the low birth rate last year. "Of course, we can't tell people to 'breed and multiply,' but we can make a better environment for people to have children."

Extension of Day Care

22 Accordingly, the Government will soon start its program of family subsidies for each pre-school child and also increase subsidies for day-care programs.

The Government also plans longer hours for 23,000 Government-supported day-care centers, with some to stay open until 10 P.M.

23 Local governments are going further, offering their own subsidies and campaigns. Yamaguchi Prefecture in rural western Japan recently launched "Operation Stork," with television commercials and postcards bearing slogans like, "Get a brother (or sister) for your child."

24 Most public surveys show that Japanese are unmoved by such steps. The Government has responded by showing some appreciation of the complex nature of the problem, and it has suggested steps to improve housing, encourage maternity leaves and permit men to come home earlier from work.

25 But few think these ideas will materialize soon. Not the least of the problems is the view that husbands in Japan work long hours and weekends, not simply because of job pressures but because they enjoy the companionship of male colleagues more than what many now commonly call "home service."

'Silent Resistance'

26 Feminists say men's attitudes are improving but that deep-rooted cultural traditions die hard.

27 "The problem is that our entire social system fails to accommodate mothers with babies," said Yuriko Marumoto, a physician, working mother and feminist, who sees the low birth rate as reflecting a "silent resistance by women" to the male-dominated system.

28 Dr. Marumoto is also one of a small band of women who have spoken out against the Government's bonuses as a repressive response devised by males.

29 "Our politicians and business leaders only go home late at night," she said, taking time out from her work at a maternity hospital. "They don't know how kids are raised, or what family life is like. Our political system is controlled by men who know nothing about the kitchen or the home."

---

*The prince did finally win his princess. Crown Prince Naruhito married Masako Owanda. The 29-year-old former career woman, a Harvard University graduate, left her job at the North America Section of Japan's Foreign Ministry to become Crown Princess Masako.

Comprehension

True/False

Decide whether each statement is true or false according to the information in the article. Then put T (true) or F (false) in the blank to the left of the question number. Explain any "false" answers in the answer blanks that follow each question.

_____ 1. The Japanese government will soon offer $152 a month to any mother with three preschool children.

_____

_____

_____ 2. Japan is unique in the world in experiencing a declining birthrate.

_____

_____

_____ 3. Unlike the United States and other places, Japan and Sweden are countries where men and women seldom live together before marriage.

_____

_____

_____ 4. This is not the first time in Japan's history that women have been pressured to have children.

_____

_____

_____ 5. Job pressure is the only reason Japanese men work long hours and weekends.

_____

_____

Comprehension

Questions and Discussion (Written or Oral)

Answer the following questions based on the information in the article.

1. Explain why Japanese women see the government's population drive as a "test of their freedom."

2. In your own words, explain how a declining birthrate would affect Japan's economy.

3. In modern industrial societies, "social security systems are taking the place of children caring for their aging parents" (par. 11). What does this mean, and how do you think it could have an impact on the birthrate?

4. " 'He was a typical Japanese man. He didn't want a partner, he wanted me to be his mother' " (par. 16). Can you *infer** from this statement that the traditional Japanese mother spoils her sons? Explain your answer.

5. A local government in Japan is calling its campaign to encourage women to have children "Operation Stork." Why do you think this name was chosen? (Look up *stork* in an unabridged (not shortened) English/English dictionary in your school library.)

6. A Japanese physician—"working mother and feminist"—"sees the low birth rate as reflecting a 'silent resistance by women' to the male-dominated system" (par. 27). Explain "silent resistance" in this context.

*****infer:** conclude; find out by reasoning

Your Opinion: Discuss or Write

How do you feel about the Japanese government's "population drive"? Do you agree with the Japanese women who are dissatisfied with their traditional roles as housewives and mothers? Why or why not?

Vocabulary Study

Guessing the Meanings of Words from Context

You shouldn't turn to your dictionary whenever you meet an unfamiliar word; it is time consuming and interrupts your train of thought. There are situations in which you will not need to know the meaning of a word to understand a sentence or a paragraph; there are times when you can guess the meaning of a word from its *context* —the words or sentences surrounding a word. The context of a word often gives you *clues* to its meaning.

Context Clues to Meaning

1. *or, that is, such as:* These words signal that the writer is defining or explaining a word.

   Examples: John always delighted in *contradicting,* or arguing exactly the opposite of, whatever the teacher said.

   Maria was an *arrogant* person; that is, she thought she was much smarter than any other person in her class.

   Some *malignancies,* such as cancer of the breast or colon, can be cured if found early.

2. *Commas, parentheses,* and *dashes* also signal definitions or explanations of words.

   Examples: There are times when you can guess the meaning of a word from its *context,* the words or sentences surrounding a word.

   There are times when you can guess the meaning of a word from its *context* (the words or sentences surrounding a word).

   There are times when you can guess the meaning of a word from its *context* — the words or sentences surrounding a word.

3. *but, although:* These words signal an opposite idea that the writer uses to define or explain a word.

   Example: Although he was a *stubborn* man, he could be flexible on occasion.

Guessing the Meanings of Words from Context

Often you can guess the meaning of a word from its *context*—the words, phrases, or sentences that surround the word. Following are some excerpts from the reading selection. Try to guess the meaning of each circled word or phrase by studying the underlined words and phrases. You may want to work with a partner.

1. "With its crowded roads, overstuffed commuter trains and cramped housing, Japan would hardly seem to be in need of more people." (par. 1)

   overstuffed* (adj.): _____

   cramped (adj.): _____

2. "So when the Government recently started telling the Japanese to bear more children, many people, especially women, became incensed." (par. 1)

   incensed (adj.): _____

3. ". . . a spreading campaign to combat a birth rate that has plummeted to its lowest level in history." (par. 2)

   plummet (v.): _____

4. "Japan's population will decline after the turn of the century, causing labor shortages, sluggish economic growth. . . ." (par. 3)

   sluggish (adj.): _____

5. ". . . their husbands work from early morning until they stagger home on the last subway train toward midnight." (par. 9)

   stagger (v.): _____

6. "They complain about . . . the drudgery of marriage to demanding husbands who do not help at home. . . ." (par. 15)

   drudgery (n.): _____

---

*Stressed syllables of the circled words are underlined.

7. "Every expert has an opinion . . . about why the <u>trend</u> [<u>low birth rate</u>] is occurring. One scholar recently suggested that <u>sports</u>, <u>video games</u> and other <u>diversions</u> were <u>robbing men</u> of their ⬭libido⬭." (par. 17)

   li<u>bi</u>do (n.): _____

8. "Accordingly, the <u>Government</u> will soon start its program of <u>family</u> ⬭subsidies⬭ for each <u>pre-school child</u> and also increase ⬭subsidies⬭ for <u>day-care programs</u>." (par. 22)

   <u>sub</u>sidy (n.): _____

9. "Feminists say men's attitudes are improving but that <u>deep-rooted cultural traditions</u> ⬭die hard⬭." (par. 26).

   die hard (idiom*): _____

10. "In Crowded <u>Japan</u>, a ⬭Bonus⬭ for <u>Babies Angers Women</u>" (title of article)

    <u>bo</u>nus (n.): _____

Prefixes

The prefixes *over-*, *pre-*, *under-*, and *ultra-* appear in the reading selection. (A prefix is a syllable or syllables put at the beginning of a word to change the meaning of the word.) In the following sentences, try to guess the meanings of the underlined words from their context. Then write the definitions in the answer blanks.

1. <u>Overloading</u> a washing machine is not good for the clothes or the machine.

   overloading: _____

2. When you look at a tired parent, you see an <u>overactive</u> child.

   overactive: _____

3. "With its crowded roads, <u>overstuffed</u> commuter trains . . ." (par. 1)

   overstuffed: _____

The prefix *over-* means _____

---

*idiom: An idiom is an expression whose meaning cannot be understood from the meaning of each word in the expression.
        Example: He failed all his courses because he didn't crack a book. <u>Crack a book</u> = open a book to study.

1. In order to save time, Americans eat a lot of <u>precooked</u> frozen foods.

   precooked: _____

2. The dinosaur was a <u>prehistoric</u> animal.

   prehistoric: _____

3. ". . . each child of <u>pre-school</u> age . . ." (par. 2)

   pre-school: _____

The prefix *pre-* means _____

1. He wanted to play basketball, but he was <u>undersized</u>.

   undersized: _____

2. I think the salesperson <u>undercharged</u> me for the sweater; I must take it back to the store.

   undercharged: _____

3. "Countering their view are feminists and family-planning experts who find it absurd to be concerned about <u>underpopulation</u>." (par. 4)

   underpopulation: _____

The prefix *under-* means _____

1. Some women think that being <u>ultrathin</u> is beautiful.

   ultrathin: _____

2. John's obsession was <u>ultracleanliness</u>; he took six showers a day.

   ultracleanliness: _____

3. "The plummeting birth rate is cited darkly by <u>ultranationalists</u>, who speak of sapping Japan's 'ethnic vitality.'" (par. 19)

   ultranationalist: _____

The prefix *ultra-* means _____

Note: Some prefixes, like some words, can have more than one meaning.

Examples: overcoat (What does *over-* mean here?)

undershirt (What does *under-* mean here?)

Glossary

A glossary is a list of the difficult words in a text and their definitions. Use the glossaries in this book as you would a dictionary.

The numbers in front of the words in the lists indicate the paragraphs (in the readings) in which the words are found. Stressed syllables are underlined.

(4)	counter (v.)	oppose
(4)	absurd (adj.)	foolish; ridiculous
(10)	militant (adj.)	active and aggressive
(10)	disenchantment (n.)	disappointment
(17)	bemoan (v.)	complain about
(20)	skyrocket (v.)	rise or increase rapidly
(20)	coercive (adj.)	using force

2. China, with Ever More to Feed, Pushes Anew for Small Families

(by Sheryl WuDunn, New York Times)

Preparing to Read

Skimming

Skim the following newspaper article and then answer the skimming questions. Look at the *title,* the *subtitle,* and the *headings.* Then read the *first two paragraphs* and the *beginnings* of the *remaining paragraphs.* Read quickly, concentrate, and take no longer than three minutes.

Skimming Questions (Do not look back at the article.)

1. China's family planning policy = heartbreak. Explain.

   _____

   _____

2. According to the article, why does the Chinese government feel it must have a family planning policy?

   _____

   _____

BEFORE YOU READ THE ARTICLE THROUGH, THINK ABOUT THE AN-SWERS TO THE FOLLOWING QUESTIONS.

— Does your country have a family planning policy? If so, why?

— Is abortion legal in your country? Are you "pro-choice" or "pro-life"? (What does the prefix *pro-* mean?)

China, With Ever More to Feed, Pushes Anew for Small Families

By SHERYL WuDUNN
Special to The New York Times

1 GUANGAN, China — Throughout China's vast countryside, it is often not so much democracy that stirs emotions as it is the desire to procreate, and few policies cause more heartbreak than the Government's family planning measures.

2 These days there are signs that the one-child policy will be carried out more rigorously. The number of women of child-bearing age is climbing dramatically, leading China to exceed its population targets, and the Government is now calling for tougher enforcement of family planning measures.

3 Here in Sichuan Province, as in most of the nation's countryside, population control has caused a mixture of anger, support, frustration, enthusiasm, deviousness and pain. Many Chinese intellectuals endorse the policy and believe it has given new hope for their country's long-term development, but it has also ruined marriages, intensified sexist attitudes and led to murder, bribery, abandonment and countless battles between mothers and daughters-in-laws.

4 "Sometimes the women cry, sometimes they don't," said a woman from Chuan Shi village, here in Guangan County, as she described the pressure on women to have abortions. "They dispatch more than a dozen people to your house all at once. They don't beat you, but they scold you, and many women are scared and just go to the hospital."

5 The case of Qi Yongxin, a peasant in Donglou village in Henan, shows how deep passions can run. When his wife became pregnant a year ago with his fourth child, a neighbor reported her to the authorities. The officials then pressured her to abort it, and Mr. Qi, his father and sister were so enraged that they beat the neighbor to death and crippled his wife and three-year-old child.

Rationed Babies
China's Population Agony

6 Mr. Qi was sentenced to death in March, according to the Peasants Daily, which reported the incident.

7 There have long been criticisms abroad of China's one-child policy, and the United States has suspended its contribution to the United Nations Family Planning Program because of allegations that the program was bolstering a coercive policy in China.*

8 But the family planning policy has made substantial progress over the last dozen years, with the average number of babies per woman dropping from five or six in 1970 to two or three now. Without population control, 240 million more Chinese babies would have been born over the last two decades, official reports say.

9 Soaring populations and insufficient farmland are a major problem in many developing countries, and supporters of the program say that China has come to grips with the problem better than most—giving its present and future generations a greater opportunity to rise above the poverty and misery that traditionally was often their lot. Most urban Chinese now seem to accept the idea that they can have only one child, and even in the countryside people desire fewer children than their parents had, although they still frequently want more than the Government allows.

10 Some Chinese describe the policy in terms that Americans might use about the income tax: fundamentally necessary, but they would rather it not apply to them personally. Still, others say that in many rural areas, where people are less educated, the policy is simply unpopular.

2.25 Children Per Woman

11 The one-child policy is a misnomer in many cases, because there are many exceptions and Chinese women have, on average, 2.25 children. Partly because the average is so much higher than one, the Government has had to abandon its original projections.

12 China is now expected to break the 1.2 billion barrier by 1995, and to approach 1.3 billion by the year 2000, the official newspapers announced in

---

*Since this article was written, the United States has resumed contributing to the U.N.'s population fund.

April. In contrast, the Government originally planned to keep the population below 1.2 billion by the year 2000.

13 China's population is now about 1.14 billion, in a territory slightly larger than the United States, but with far less arable land.

14 Will the missed targets prompt a new crackdown? So far, the Government has called for tighter controls, and there seems to be a greater attempt to raise fines for evasion and to limit the number of cases where second and third children are allowed.

More Money Sought

15 Official press reports have also called for more spending on family planning, which currently receives less than one percent of the central budget. But so far officials deny that a new crackdown is imminent, and there is no sign of another "high tide" of the kind that a decade ago led to many forced abortions in Chinese villages.

16 Peasants, officials and others interviewed during a weeklong tour of Sichuan Province, and in other parts of China in recent months, said that it was quite rare for the authorities to drag a woman to the hospital to undergo an abortion, but that it still happened.

17 "Last year there was a forced abortion in my village," said a young woman from Hongjiang Village in Sichuan. "More than a dozen cadres went to the woman's house and forced her to go to the hospital for the abortion."

18 Officials do not disclose national statistics on forced abortion, but Zeng Jian, the director of family planning for Guangan, said that in 1990, the county had "about 100 forced abortions." This represented about 3 percent of 3,200 abortions that took place in the county in 1990. The phrase in Chinese that Mr. Zeng used normally suggests compulsion or physical force, rather than simply pressure tactics.

19 He added that last year, Guangan, with 1.09 million people, had only 200 unauthorized births, compared to 15,000 within the plan.

20 Peasants also described other tactics, such as demolishing houses, confiscating furniture or electrical appliances, or beating the husbands of those who violate the policy.

21 Both officials and many peasants, however, say such methods are used infrequently. Indeed, visits to villages in many parts of China suggest that unauthorized children are far more common than destroyed houses. It is common in some rural areas to see couples with three children, occasionally even four, and local officials are often willing to charge a fine and look the other way.

22 "If they refuse to pay the fine, their radio set and TV may be taken as mortgage — yes, I've seen this in some places, but it is quite rare," said Shen Guoxiang, the spokesman for the State Family Planning Commission in Beijing.

23 The most common way of persuading couples to have fewer children is simply to offer a series of incentives and fines, and if these fail, to turn to pressure tactics aimed at making people feel guilty if they breach the policy. Here in Sichuan, which has a population of 108 million, one-child families get a wide range of benefits. These vary but can include monthly subsidies of $1, higher retirement pensions for the parents, greater allocation of land, lower grain taxes and easier access to good schools.

24 A fine for a child born out of the plan can amount to up to two years' income, but villages tend to set their own fines. Some even offer installment plans for families that cannot pay the fine in one lump sum.

Monitoring System

25 The incentives are linked to an efficient monitoring system—which includes about 13 million volunteers—intended to detect pregnancies as soon as possible. In Guangan, villages and townships keep lists of all the women of child-bearing age, and oblige them to undergo gynecological check-ups every three months—apparently to insure that no one conceals a pregnancy.

26 One of the most effective methods of preventing unauthorized pregnancies is obligatory sterilization of couples who have already had two or more children. But it is common for mothers to flee their villages when they are summoned for sterilization or when they are expecting a baby outside of the plan.

27 In Guangdong's Wuhua County, last July's census workers discovered that over the years nearly 38,000 children had secretly been born and not registered with the authorities, according to a recent report in the Nanfang Daily.

28 The most common reason for couples to breach the policy is that they want a son, to continue the family name and ancestry. In Chinese tradition, daughters are married out of the family, while sons remain to care for their parents in their old age. So parents often keep having children until they have a son.

Scanning

Skimming is reading quickly to get the *general idea* of a reading selection.
Scanning is reading quickly to find *specific information*. When you look up a telephone number in the directory or look up a word in the dictionary, are you *skimming* or *scanning?*
Scan the article you have just read for the following information and write it on the blank lines.

1. Why Mr. Qi, his father, and his sister beat their neighbor to death (You will very quickly search for *Mr. Qi* and then answer the question.)

    _____

2. Results of population control since 1970 (Quickly find *1970.*)

    _____

3. Projected population in China by the year 2000

    _____

4. Why "one-child policy" is a misnomer in many cases

    _____

5. How China compares in size and in arable land with the United States

    _____

6. a.   Number of abortions in county of Guangan in 1990
   b.   Number of forced abortions in same county, same year

_____

7. Purpose of the monitoring system

_____

8. Most common reason for couples to violate the one-child policy

_____

Comprehension

Questions and Discussion (Written or Oral)

1. Both China and Japan are concerned about the birthrate in their respective countries. *Contrast* their concerns, and *compare* and *contrast* the manner in which they are dealing with these concerns.

2. Why would the well-educated Chinese and the Chinese peasants feel differently about their government's one-child policy?

3. Explain in your own words the following excerpt from paragraph 10 of the article: "Some Chinese describe the policy in terms that Americans might use about the income tax: fundamentally necessary, but they would rather it not apply to them personally."

4. "It is common in some rural areas to see couples with three children, occasionally even four, and local officials are often willing to charge a fine and look the other way" (par. 21). Explain "look the other way." What does this *imply** about some local officials?

5. About 13 million volunteers help implement the monitoring system. What does this mean, and why do you think these millions of people volunteer their services? (Be sure you know what the words *volunteer* and *implement* mean.)

6. In *your own words,* restate the title and the subtitle of the article you have just read.

---

*imply: express indirectly; suggest

Your Opinion: Discuss or Write

Do you think that the Chinese government's "family planning measures" are *justified?* Explain your answer. Do you approve of these measures? Why or why not? What do you think is the answer to *overpopulation?*

Vocabulary Study

Guessing the Meanings of Words from Context

Following are some excerpts from the reading selection. Try to guess the meaning of each circled word by studying the underlined words and phrases. You may want to work with a partner.

1. "These days there are signs that the <u>one-child policy will be carried out</u> more (rigorously.) . . . the Government is now calling for <u>tougher enforcement</u> of family planning measures." (par. 2)

    <u>rig</u>orously* (adv.): _____

2. "Many Chinese intellectuals (endorse) the policy and believe it has <u>given new hope for their country's long-term development</u>. . . ." (par. 3)

    en<u>dorse</u> (v.): _____

3. "'They (dispatch) more than a <u>dozen people to your house</u> all at once. They <u>don't beat you</u>, but they (scold) you, and many <u>women are scared</u>. . . .'" (par. 4)

    dis<u>patch</u> (v.): _____

    scold (v.): _____

4. "When his wife became <u>pregnant</u> . . . a neighbor reported her to the authorities. The <u>officials</u> then <u>pressured</u> her to (abort) it, and Mr. Qi, his father and sister were so (enraged) that <u>they beat the neighbor to death</u>. . . ." (par. 5)

    a<u>bort</u> (v.): _____

    en<u>raged</u> (adj.): _____

5. "(Soaring) <u>populations and insufficient farmland</u> are a <u>major problem</u> in many developing countries. . . ." (par. 9)

    <u>soar</u>ing (adj.): _____

_____
*Stressed syllables of the circled words are underlined.

6. "The <u>one-child policy</u> is a⟨misnomer⟩in many cases, because there are <u>many exceptions</u> and <u>Chinese women have, on average, 2.25 children</u>." (par. 11)

    mis<u>no</u>mer (n.): _____

    (Hint: the prefix *mis-* means *wrong*.)

7. "So far, the Government has called for <u>tighter controls</u>, and there seems to be a greater attempt to <u>raise</u>⟨fines⟩for⟨evasion⟩and to <u>limit the number of cases where second and third children are allowed</u>." (par. 14)

    fine (n.): _____

    e<u>va</u>sion (n.): _____

    (Hint: Have you ever had to pay a *fine* for speeding?)

8. "The incentives are linked to an efficient⟨monitoring⟩system — which includes about <u>13 million volunteers</u> — intended to⟨detect⟩<u>pregnancies as soon as possible</u>." (par. 25)

    <u>mo</u>nitoring (adj.): _____

    de<u>tect</u> (v.): _____

9. "One of the most effective methods of <u>preventing unauthorized pregnancies</u> is⟨obligatory⟩<u>sterilization of couples</u>. . . ." (par. 26)

    o<u>bli</u>gatory (adj.): _____

10. "The most common <u>reason for couples</u> to⟨breach⟩the <u>policy</u> is that they want a <u>son to continue the family name and ancestry</u>." (par. 28)

    breach (v.): _____

Glossary

The numbers in front of the words indicate the paragraphs (in the reading) in which the words are found. Stressed syllables are underlined.

(1)	<u>pro</u>create (v.)	produce offspring, children
(2)	ex<u>ceed</u> (v.)	to go beyond
(3)	frus<u>tra</u>tion (n.)	disappointment, dissatisfaction
(3)	<u>de</u>viousness (n.)	dishonesty

(3)	<u>brib</u>ery (n.)	giving or taking gifts to influence someone to do wrong
(7)	alle<u>ga</u>tion (n.)	a statement that accuses someone of doing something bad but that is not supported by truth
(9)	lot (n.)	fate, fortune, or destiny
(13)	<u>ar</u>able (adj.)	used to describe land suitable for growing crops
(14)	<u>crack</u>down (n.)	a severe enforcing of laws
(15)	<u>im</u>minent (adj.)	likely to happen soon
(17)	<u>ca</u>dre (n.)	a small group of trained workers in a communist country
(20)	<u>con</u>fiscate (v.)	to seize (private property) officially and without payment
(23)	allo<u>ca</u>tion	the setting apart for a particular purpose

3. It May Not Be Too Late for the World to Come to Grips with Overpopulation

(by Myrne Roe, Wichita Eagle*)*

Preparing to Read

Skimming

Skim the following article by Myrne Roe. Look at the *title*. Read the *first* and *last paragraphs* and the *first sentence* of *each intervening paragraph*.

Recognizing the Topic

What do you think this article is about? What is the *subject* or *topic* of the article?

a. population growth
b. overpopulation
c. the world's population
d. family planning

Note: The topic is usually expressed in a word or phrase, not a sentence.

NOW READ THE ARTICLE THROUGH.

Myrne Roe
It may not be too late for the world to come to grips with overpopulation

1   WICHITA, Kan.—Anyone who plans to be around in 40 years should be more than a little concerned that by that time the world's population will double if the current birth rate isn't slowed significantly. And those whose kids and grandkids will be around then should be troubled that in 2033 the planet Earth probably won't be able to support all those humans living on it.

2   According to the Population Institute, a non-profit educational organization specializing in global population issues, every 10 minutes 2,400 more babies are born. Half of them are born in nations where natural and economic resources are already limited by too many people. In the year 2020, the combined populations of Asia and Africa alone will be 6 billion to 8 billion, more than the current population of 5.6 billion for the entire world.

3   There are already 65 countries that depend on subsistence farming and by the year 2000 won't be able to feed their people. Despite an epidemic of AIDS and increasing starvation, death rates won't even get close to current birth rates.

4   And since 70 percent of Third World families depend on wood for fuel, the specter of continued deforestation and its resulting devastation to the world's ecological systems is ominous. It is estimated that by the year 2000 timberland equaling the size of 40 Californias will disappear. Also by 2000, the world will have to produce 800 million new jobs to accommodate the population growth.

5   In human terms, continuing overpopulation will lead to more and more of the world's people living a life of hunger, cold and poverty. More and more wars will be fought over less and less land. And there will eventually be what Werner Fornos, the head of the Population Institute, calls "an environmental apocalypse."

6   Where there has been political leadership, there have been tremendous inroads into slowing out-of-control birth rates. In Mexico, for example, 65 percent of all couples use birth control after the government set up family planning clinics and launched

---

In human terms, continuing overpopulation will lead to more and more of the world's people living a life of hunger, cold and poverty.

---

an information campaign. From 1970 to 1975, the population growth there was higher than it is in Africa today. But the numbers have dropped from 6.75 children per woman to today's average of 3.8 children per woman.

7   For those who think that as long as they, their kids and grandkids live in the good old U.S.A. there's no reason to get excited, think again. In America, the population is expected to grow by 52 percent by 2050. And 23 percent of those now giving birth are teenagers; 60 percent of them live on Aid to Families with Dependent Children.

8   In addition, this nation, which currently makes up only 5 percent of the world's population, uses 30 percent of the world's resources. By the time a child born in this country today reaches age 75, he or she will produce 52 tons of garbage and consume 10 million gallons of water. So adding more and more Americans to the world's population adds more and more environmental problems, too.

9   For 12 years, the United States did very little to support worldwide efforts to cope with overpopulation. Now the Clinton administration has taken steps—and Congress has agreed—to once again contribute money to the U.N.'s population fund. President Clinton, in his recent speech to the U.N., said: "Our nation has, at last, renewed its commitment to expand the availability of the world's family planning education and service. We must ensure that there is a place at the table for every one of our world's children. And we can do it."

10   He's right. It can be done. But it will take political courage and considerable dollars to educate the world's women about birth control, and make it available to them. And the world's men must learn to accept their share of the responsibility for birth control and parenting, as well.

11   With 2,400 babies born every 10 minutes for the next 40 years, the future for everyone's kids and grandkids is downright bleak. As a headline in a Population Institute publication put it: "No matter what your cause—it's a lost cause if we don't come to grips with overpopulation."—(c1993.)

Myrne Roe is an editorial writer for The Wichita (Kan.) Eagle.

Comprehension

Recognizing the Main Idea

What is the *main idea* or the *main point* of Ms. Roe's article? What is the writer saying about the topic? What point is she making about the topic? (Refer to "Recognizing the Topic" on p. 23.) In a sentence or two, write the main idea of the article.

_____

_____

_____

True/False

Scan the article for the answers to the following true/false statements. Then put T (true) or F (false) in the blanks to the left of the question numbers. Explain any "false" answers in the answer blanks that follow each question.

_____ 1. The reader can conclude that if nothing is done to curb the birth rate, by 2033 the world's population will number 11.2 billion.

_____

_____

_____ 2. In Asia and Africa alone, 2,400 babies are born every 10 minutes.

_____

_____

_____ 3. The AIDS epidemic and starvation will most likely kill so many people that the death rate will soon catch up with the birth rate.

_____

_____

_____ 4. "Third World" in paragraph 4 refers to countries that contain one-third of the world's population.

_____

_____

_____ 5. By the year 2000, California will be completely deforested.

_____

_____

_____ 6. America's population will more than double by the year 2050.

_____

_____

_____ 7. 60 percent of births in the United States are to the poor.

_____

_____

_____ 8. An affluent nation, such as the United States, would be more likely to deplete the world's resources than the poorer nations.

_____

_____

_____ 9. The United States has promised to do its part in controlling world population.

_____

_____

_____ 10. The reader can **infer** from this article that men and women have always shared equally in the responsibility of birth control.

_____

_____

Reading Critically

Reading critically is making judgments about what you have read. The following questions will help guide you in making some judgments about Myrne Roe's article.

— Why do you think Ms. Roe wrote about overpopulation? What was her purpose?

— Whom do you think Ms. Roe wrote this article for? Did she have a specific audience in mind?

— Where did the writer get her information? Do you think the statistics she quotes are reliable?

— Do you think the writer has credibility? Do you think she is qualified to write about this subject? What is her profession?

— Do you think Myrne Roe accomplished her purpose? Explain your answer.

Vocabulary Study

Guessing the Meanings of Words from Context

Following are some excerpts from the reading selection. In the guessing-from-context exercises in chapters 1 and 2, the underlined words and phrases helped you guess the meanings of unfamiliar words. Now *you* will underline the words and phrases that will help you guess the meaning of each circled word or phrase. Be sure to work with a partner.

1. *Example:*   ". . . in 40 years . . . the <u>world's population</u> will <u>double</u> if the <u>current birth rate isn't slowed</u> (significantly)." (par. 1)

    si<u>gnif</u>icantly* (adv.): _____

2. "Despite an (epidemic) of AIDS and increasing starvation, death rates won't even get close to current birth rates." (par. 3)

    epi<u>dem</u>ic (n.): _____

3. "And since 70 percent of Third World families depend on wood for fuel, the specter of continued (deforestation) and its resulting devastation to the world's ecological systems is ominous." (par. 4) (Hint: What does the prefix *de-* mean?)

    defores<u>ta</u>tion (n.): _____

4. "By the time a child born in this country today reaches age 75, he or she will produce 52 tons of garbage and (consume) 10 million gallons of water." (par. 8)

    con<u>sume</u> (v.): _____

5. "'Our nation has, at last, renewed its commitment to expand the availability of the world's family planning education and service. We must ensure that there is (a place at the table) for every one of our world's children. . . .'" (par. 9)

    a place at the table (idiom): _____

6. "With 2,400 babies born every 10 minutes for the next 40 years, the future for everyone's kids and grandkids is downright (bleak)." (par. 11)

    bleak (adj.): _____

---

*Stressed syllables of the circled words are underlined.

Glossary

The numbers in front of the words indicate the paragraphs (in the reading) in which the words are found. Stressed syllables are underlined.

(3)	sub<u>sis</u>tence <u>farm</u>ing	farming whose products are intended to provide for the basic needs of the farmer, with little surplus for marketing
(4)	<u>spec</u>ter (n.)	some object or source of terror or dread
(4)	devas<u>ta</u>tion (n.)	destruction
(4)	eco<u>log</u>ical (adj.)	pertaining to the relationship between organisms and their environment
(4)	<u>om</u>inous (adj.)	threatening
(5)	a<u>poc</u>alypse (n.)	any universal or widespread destruction or disaster
(11)	come to grips with (idiom)	deal with

Review: Vocabulary

Recalling Content through Vocabulary

The following vocabulary should help you recall something about the content of the readings in Unit 1. What does each of these vocabulary items help you remember about the readings? Do not look back at the readings.

Example: agony: Some Chinese women are suffering greatly because of their government's one-child policy.

1. come to grips with: _____

2. cramped: _____

3. disenchantment: _____

4. dispatch: _____

5. misnomer: _____

6. overpopulation: _____

7. plummet: _____

8. rationed: _____

9. sluggish: _____

Review: Vocabulary

Fill in each blank in the following sentences with the appropriate word from the list. Use the correct tenses of the verbs.

absurd	crackdown	scold
arable	detect	significantly
bleak	drudgery	soar
bonus	imminent	stagger
breach	obligatory	ultrarich
coercive	overeat	underfed
consume	plummet	

1. The prices of consumer goods have _____, forcing many people to

    cut down on their spending.

2. There has been a _____ on drunk drivers.

3. Before one boards an airplane, it is _____ to pass through a metal

    detector.

4. In the fall of the year, the temperature can _____ from very warm

    to very cold.

5. Because he had been ill for over a month, he _____ as if he were

    drunk.

6. Many of the _____ donate millions of dollars to the needy.

7. Mrs. Brown _____ her little boy for running into the street.

8. Because Brenda was a hard worker, her boss gave her a _____ at the end of the year.

9. It is no longer _____ to think that a woman may one day be president of the United States.

10. Richard was heartbroken after Linda _____ her promise to marry him.

11. There are many _____ children among the poor.

12. John gained weight because he _____.

13. Lung cancer would decrease _____ if everyone stopped smoking.

14. Some students consider studying a _____; others consider it a pleasure.

15. The little boy _____ five candy bars in one afternoon.

16. Diplomacy failed to settle the dispute between the two countries; now war seemed _____.

17. I _____ her sadness when I saw tears in her eyes.

18. Those who drop out of school have _____ futures.

19. There was very little to eat because much of the land was not _____.

20. Do you think a government has the right to use _____ measures to curb population growth?

Review: Vocabulary

Put an ✕ in front of any statement that does not make good sense.

Example: _✕_ Nancy received a bonus because her boss was dissatisfied with her work.

_____ 1. He had to pay a fine for illegal parking.

_____ 2. Maria was unable to have a child because she was fertile.

_____ 3. Joe's mother scolded him because he always did his homework and made A's on his tests.

_____ 4. Prices skyrocketed and everyone had to be careful about spending.

_____ 5. Because she was disenchanted with marriage, she wanted to find a husband.

_____ 6. Brian became enraged when someone broke into his house and stole his television and VCR.

4. The 1990 Census: An American Self-Portrait

(by Karin C. Rosenberg, The World Book*)*

Preparing to Read

THINK ABOUT THE ANSWERS TO THE FOLLOWING QUESTIONS.

— Define *census*.

— How often is the census taken in your country?

— Do the majority of people in your country live in cities or in small towns and villages?

— Is the population of your country a mix of different racial or ethnic groups?

— What is the present population of your country? Has there been an increase or decrease in population over the past 10 years?

— How many people make up a typical household in your country? Explain.

Note: If you had trouble answering some of these questions, look up the answers in an encyclopedia in your school library.

Skimming

Take a few minutes to skim the article from the encyclopedia *The World Book*. Read the *title* and the *sentence in large print below the author's name*. Then read the *first paragraph*, the *first sentence or two* of the *succeeding paragraphs,* and the *entire last paragraph*. Look quickly at the *graphs* on page 39.

Answer the following skimming questions without looking back at the article.

1. Define *census*.

_____

2. The official reason for the United States census is
   a. to project population growth in the next 10 years
   b. to check up on illegal immigrants
   c. to determine how many representatives each state will send to the House of Representatives

3. *Demography* is the study of
   a. the geography of a country
   b. population trends
   c. the United States government

4. The fastest growing generation in the 1980s was
   a. the baby boomers
   b. people of color
   c. age 65 and older

5. Blacks make up what percentage of the U.S. population?
   a. 50 percent
   b. 12 percent
   c. 3 percent

NOW READ THE ARTICLE THROUGH.

The 1990 Census: An American Self-Portrait

By Karin C. Rosenberg

The latest figures from the United States Bureau of the Census reveal a changing picture of who Americans are and where and how they live.

1 Every 10 years since 1790, the United States has taken an inventory of its inhabitants known as the Census of Population. The official reason for taking a census is to determine the number of seats each state will fill in the U.S. House of Representatives. But the census serves many other purposes as well. One of its most important functions is to provide a picture of who Americans are and where and how they live. Over the past 200 years, census statistics have measured America's growth and reflected shifts in living patterns.

2 For example, census data have charted America's shift from an overwhelmingly rural society to one that is predominantly urban. In 1790, only 1 American in 20 lived in an urban area, defined by the U.S. Bureau of the Census as a town or city of 2,500 or more people. Not until the 1920 census did urban residents overtake rural residents. By 1990, urban residents outnumbered rural residents 3 to 1.

3 The United States reached another milestone in 1990: For the first time, more than half the U.S. population lived in large metropolitan areas of more than a million people. During the 1980's, these metropolitan areas experienced steady growth on their fringes. As in the past, urban sprawl advanced as people moved to more and more distant suburbs to find affordable housing. At the same time, small towns were disappearing. Nearly three-quarters of U.S. towns with fewer than 2,500 inhabitants lost population during the 1980's, more than in any previous decade.

4 Another trend the 1990 census spotted was the growth of the suburban city: Of the 29 cities that surpassed the 100,000 population mark for the first time, 22 were suburbs of larger cities. These so-called satellite cities offered jobs as well as shopping and cultural activities. It has become increasingly common for people to both live and work in the suburbs.

5 Population growth, according to *demographers* (people who study population trends), usually indicates that an area is economically healthy. People tend to stay in or move to areas where jobs are available. And companies that hire new employees generally tend to be profitable.

6 Since the 1950 census, the Northeastern and Midwestern sections of the United States have grown far more slowly than have the Southern and Western regions. Industrial cities in the North have been hit especially hard, as the heavy industries on which they long depended have become less important to the U.S. economy. At the same time, the South and West have grown phenomenally, picking up nearly 90 per cent of America's population gain in the 1980's.

7 More than half the U.S. population growth from 1980 to 1990 occurred in just three states—California, Florida, and Texas. By 1990, 1 in 8 Americans lived in California, the nation's most populous state, and California's 29.8 million people surpassed Canada's entire population of 26.3 million. These population shifts foretell a dramatic swing in economic and political power from the Frostbelt to the Sunbelt.

8 Other shifts recorded by the 1990 census also point toward future social and political directions. For example, America is becoming more ethnically and racially diverse as its minorities increase faster than the population as a whole. By 1990, 1 in 4 Americans considered themselves nonwhite or Hispanic, according to census forms. In 1980, only 1 in 5 did.

9   This increased diversity also reflects how Americans see themselves. In 1990, the census recorded a big jump in the Native American population, which now numbers 1.8 million, three times its size in 1960. Experts theorize that many people who hid their Indian ancestry in the past now claim it proudly. Questions about Hispanic ancestry first appeared on the 1980 census in response to requests by Hispanic leaders. Hispanics, who make up 9 per cent of the U.S. population, are not considered a separate racial group, however. They may belong to white, black, or Indian racial groups.

10   A group to watch is the enormous generation born from 1946 through 1964, during the so-called baby boom. Baby boomers make up nearly a third of the nation's people and exert a powerful influence on American society. When they were young, during the 1960's and 1970's, they gave America the youth culture, the anti-war movement, and the phrase "Never trust anyone over 30." Baby boomers by 1990 had begun to enter middle age, and the nation has become preoccupied with health and fitness.

11   But the fastest-growing generation during the 1980's was age 65 and older. By 1990, a record number of Americans—12.5 per cent of the population—were retirement age. Demographers expect growth of this group to slow in the 1990's, however, when people born during the Great Depression of the 1930's begin to turn 65. Birth rates plunged during the depression as people's expectations for the future fell.

12   Changes in smaller groups also emerge from census data. In 1790, U.S. families had an average of nearly six members. An average U.S.

Getting the numbers

In March 1990, the Bureau of the Census mailed out nearly 90 million census forms to addresses across America. Much effort had gone into compiling the address lists, largely through purchases from firms that specialize in drawing up mailing lists. Census takers and postal workers dropped off census forms at millions of additional households, mainly those in rural areas without street addresses. In all, more than 100 million homes across America received 1990 census forms.

The Census Bureau prints two kinds of questionnaires. About 5 out of 6 households receive a short form with 14 questions. Half the questions ask about the age, sex, ancestry, marital status, and relationship of the household's residents. The other half relate to housing conditions, such as the number of rooms in a dwelling and whether the dwelling is owned or rented. Only 1 household in 6 receives a long form that asks 19 additional questions; for example, what kind of work the residents do; how they commute to work; and what, if any, disabilities they have.

The forms were due back on April 1. Processing began immediately, with clerical workers and computers checking forms for completeness. Census takers made follow-up telephone calls to obtain any missing information, such as children's ages. They also phoned or visited those who failed to return census forms. Neighbors were sometimes interviewed to obtain information on absent residents. Finally, local governments had an opportunity to review counts and to identify discrepancies between census lists and local records.

To achieve as accurate a count as possible, in 1990 the Census Bureau made its first effort to include Americans who have no homes. On the night of March 20, 1990, census takers in cities across the nation counted people spending the night in shelters for the homeless or sleeping in doorways, parks, abandoned buildings, and other such places. Census officials emphasized that the homeless count of 229,000 was far from inclusive, though it marked a start in the difficult task of locating the nation's homeless.

Once the census forms were completed, cameras photographed them on microfilm, and optical scanning devices transferred the information on the film to a computer tape. Computers then tabulated the information. The Census Bureau began releasing complete counts as they became available. But all the information from the long forms was not due out before late 1993.

household in 1990, with 2.63 people, was less than half that size. Moreover, today's households are far less likely than ever before to consist of a married couple and their children. Before 1990, this traditional family group had always outnumbered other types of households in the United States. But the 1990 census found that married couples who lived without children—either because they had none or because their children were grown—formed the nation's most common household unit.

13 As households have shrunk in size, their number has proliferated. Divorce has created additional, smaller households, as has the tendency of young people to live alone and marry late. All these new households have required new housing, which for some years fueled the construction industry and real estate market.

14 The census breaks down population information by age, sex, and language, among other factors. Such information helps urban planners determine where to locate new schools, roads, hospitals, housing, and other facilities. Knowing how many Spanish-speaking preschoolers live in a particular school district, for example, could help school boards set hiring policies for teachers and decide where new elementary schools are needed. Similarly, a jump in a community's elderly population may indicate a need for more hospitals and public transportation. Some small towns seek to offset population losses by recruiting residents from America's many retirees, offering them a crime-free, low-cost place to live.

15 Businesses use census data to identify markets for their products or services. Many businesses would like to cash in on the enormous baby-boom market now approaching middle age. Opticians can expect to profit as baby boomers require reading glasses. Publishers may target this generation with more magazines that offer information on health and fitness or advice on investments. Other businesses have looked at the nation's expanding ethnic diversity to find new markets. For example, large cosmetics firms that previously targeted only whites have announced plans to bring out new lines aimed at blacks and Hispanics.

16 The most important uses of the census, however, go beyond spotting trends. Population figures determine how much federal funding the states and cities receive for such crucial budget items as education, public transportation, housing, and poverty programs. Poor Americans—those who depend most heavily on government-funded programs—abound in large U.S. cities. Yet the urban poor are also the people most likely to go uncounted by the census. Because undercounting can mean cuts in government funding, census results matter greatly to cities and states.

17 In 1790—three years after its Constitution was written—the United States became the first country to establish a complete, periodic census. Once America had introduced representative government, that government needed to know whom it represented. For 200 years, the census has provided a self-portrait of America and a foundation for government by the people.

THE NEW AMERICAN MIX

Increasing diversity

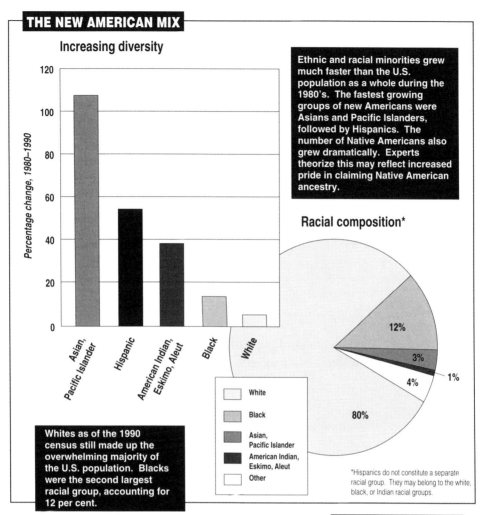

Percentage change, 1980–1990

- Asian, Pacific Islander
- Hispanic
- American Indian, Eskimo, Aleut
- Black
- White

Ethnic and racial minorities grew much faster than the U.S. population as a whole during the 1980's. The fastest growing groups of new Americans were Asians and Pacific Islanders, followed by Hispanics. The number of Native Americans also grew dramatically. Experts theorize this may reflect increased pride in claiming Native American ancestry.

Racial composition*

12%
3%
1%
4%
80%

- White
- Black
- Asian, Pacific Islander
- American Indian, Eskimo, Aleut
- Other

*Hispanics do not constitute a separate racial group. They may belong to the white, black, or Indian racial groups.

Whites as of the 1990 census still made up the overwhelming majority of the U.S. population. Blacks were the second largest racial group, accounting for 12 per cent.

Who is coming to America

Until the mid-1950's, America's immigrants arrived primarily from Europe. By 1990, at least 4 out of 5 U.S. immigrants came from non-European countries. Nearly 1 in 4 Americans claimed some African, Asian, Hispanic, or American Indian ancestry in 1990, up from 1 in 5 in 1980.

Fast-growing ethnic groups

Vietnamese	+135%
Asian Indians	+126%
Chinese	+104%
Filipinos	+82%
Mexicans	+54%
Puerto Ricans	+35%

Comprehension

True/False and Multiple Choice

Here are some questions about the article you have just read. Some are true/false; some are multiple choice. Answer as many questions as you can without looking back at the article. Then scan the reading for any information that you don't remember. Explain any "false" answers in the answer blanks that follow the true/false questions.

_____ 1.   The United States has counted its inhabitants every year for the past 200 years. (T/F)

_____

_____

_____ 2.   Although the majority of Americans live in cities, the United States has remained a rural society. (T/F)

_____

_____

_____ 3.   A satellite city is a suburb that has grown into a city. (T/F)

_____

_____

_____ 4.   Which of the following three states has the most people?
           a. California
           b. Florida
           c. Texas

_____ 5.   The reader can **infer** that the most likely reason the South and West have increased in population is that
           a. the people are friendlier in the South and West
           b. the economy is better in the South and West
           c. life is slower in the South and West

_____ 6. There was a decrease in the minority population in the United States between 1980 and 1990. (T/F)

_____

_____

_____ 7. Hispanics, like whites, blacks, and Indians, are a separate racial group. (T/F)

_____

_____

_____ 8. According to the 1990 census, the traditional household of parents and two or more children is still the most common household in America. (T/F)

_____

_____

_____ 9.   The fastest growing group of new Americans during the 1980s was
               the Hispanics. (T/F)

               _____

               _____

_____ 10.   Except for the Native Americans, America has always been a nation
               of immigrants. (T/F)

               _____

               _____

_____ 11.   The 1990 census included for the first time information about
               a.   Asians
               b.   the homeless
               c.   minorities

         12.   Define *minorities* in the context of this article.

               _____

               _____

Questions and Discussion (Written or Oral)

1. The 1990 census recorded that small towns in the United States are disappearing. "Nearly three-quarters of U.S. towns with fewer than 2,500 inhabitants lost population during the 1980's . . . ." Why do you think small towns are disappearing? Is this true in your country? Are there any advantages to living in a small town? If so, what are they?

2. From the information in paragraphs 6 and 7 in the article, you should be able to guess the meanings of *Frostbelt* and *Sunbelt*. Define each.

3. According to the census, America is becoming more ethnically diverse. What is the meaning of *ethnically diverse?* Is the population of your country culturally homogeneous? Why or why not? (Look up *homogeneous* in your English/English dictionary.)

4. Why are American Indians also referred to as Native Americans? Can you guess the difference in meaning between Native American and native American? The 1990 census shows a big jump in the Native American population. What do the experts think is the reason for this?

5. What was the Baby Boom? Why do you think there was a baby boom? (Think about the *dates* of the baby boom.) Who is the most powerful baby boomer in the United States today?

6. If you were planning to be a physician, how could census data help you decide what medical specialty (pediatrician, geriatrician, orthopedist, etc.) to choose and *where* to practice medicine?

7. Why is it very important that poor people in large cities not be undercounted?

8. What are three facts that you learned from the 1990 U.S. census that you did not know beforehand?

Vocabulary Study

Guessing the Meanings of Words from Context

Following are some excerpts from the reading selection. Try to guess the meanings of the circled words from their context. As you did in chapter 3, underline the words and phrases that will help you guess the meanings. Work with a partner.

1. *Example:* "...census data have charted America's (shift) from an (overwhelmingly) rural society to one that is (predominantly) urban. In 1790, only 1 American in 20 lived in an urban area. . . . By 1990, urban residents outnumbered rural residents 3 to 1." (par. 2)

   shift (n.): _____

   over<u>whelm</u>ingly* (adv.): _____

   pre<u>dom</u>inantly (adv.): _____

---

*Stressed syllables of the circled words are underlined.

2. "The United States reached another milestone in 1990: For the first time, more than half the U.S. population lived in large metropolitan areas of more than a million people. During the 1980's, these metropolitan areas experienced steady growth on their fringes. As in the past, urban sprawl advanced as people moved to more and more distant suburbs to find affordable housing." (par. 3)

   milestone (n.): _____

   fringes (n.): _____

   sprawl (n.): _____

3. "At the same time, the South and West have grown phenomenally, picking up nearly 90 per cent of America's population gain in the 1980's." (par. 6)

   phenomenally (adv.): _____

4. "In 1990, the census recorded a big jump in the Native American population, which now numbers 1.8 million, three times its size in 1960." (par. 9)

   jump (n.): _____

5. "As households have shrunk in size, their number has proliferated. Divorce has created additional, smaller households, as has the tendency of young people to live alone and marry late. All these new households have required new housing, . . ." (par. 13)

   proliferate (v.): _____

6. "Some small towns seek to offset population losses by recruiting residents from America's many retirees, offering them a crime-free, low-cost place to live." (par. 14)

   offset (v.): _____

   recruit (v.): _____

7. Many businesses would like to cash in on the enormous baby-boom market now approaching middle age. Opticians can expect to profit as baby boomers require reading glasses. Publishers may target this generation with more magazines that offer information on health and fitness. . . ." (par. 15)

   cash in on (idiom): _____

Prefixes

The prefix *anti-* appears in the following sentence from the reading selection. Study the sentence and then try to guess the meanings of the three words listed. Write the definitions in the answer blanks.

"When they were young, during the 1960's and 1970's, they gave America the youth culture, the *antiwar* movement, and the phrase 'Never trust anyone over 30.'" (par. 10)

antiwar: _____

antiabortion: _____

antismoking: _____

The prefix *anti-* means _____

5. In 2050 America Will Be . . .

(by Carrie Teegardin, Atlanta Journal*)*

Preparing to Read

— Skim the following article; look at the graphs. Why will America be "more crowded, more ethnic, and grayer" in 2050?

— Ask three Americans to tell you (1) what country their parents, grandparents, or ancestors came from; (2) why America is often thought of as a "melting pot."

NOW READ THE ARTICLE THROUGH.

In 2050 America will be . . .

more crowded . . .

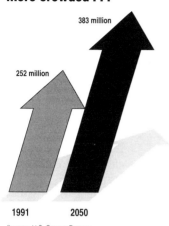

383 million

252 million

1991   2050

Source: U.S. Census Bureau

more ethnic . . .

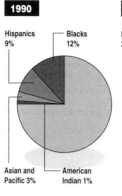

1990

Hispanics 9%   Blacks 12%

Asian and Pacific 3%   American Indian 1%

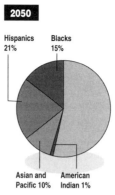

2050

Hispanics 21%   Blacks 15%

Asian and Pacific 10%   American Indian 1%

and grayer.

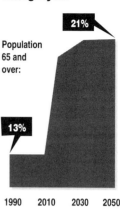

21%

Population 65 and over:

13%

1990   2010   2030   2050

Census Bureau paints America's future

Nation in 60 years will become more ethnic and more crowded

By Carrie Teegardin

STAFF WRITER

1 The year is 2050, and today's elementary school students will be hitting retirement age. They'll call their grandchildren on shirt-pocket satellite telephones, watch 3-D TV and ride in cars that drive themselves.

2 And they'll still be catering to their own doddering baby boomer parents, who will swell the over-85 age bracket as they test the limits of the human body and America's Social Security system.

3 In a report released today, U.S. Census Bureau analysts have drawn a picture of America during the next six decades that reveals a nation transformed by the effects of immigration, population growth and increasing life expectancy.

4 By 2050, the nation will be more crowded, more ethnic and living longer.

5 Census experts predict that the country will grow by 50 percent, to 383 million people, by 2050. The average person will expect to live 82 years, up from today's 76.

6 Americans of Hispanic origin will make up a larger share of the population than black people by 2050. And the Asian population will have more than quadrupled, according to the report. Only half of Americans will be white people, down from three-fourths today.

7 By projecting the latest population trends over the next six decades, the Census Bureau's report acts more as a mirror than a crystal ball.

8 There is no attempt to predict another baby boom, an end to America's popularity with immigrants, or a reduction in the birthrate. Instead, the report shows what the future will be like if the near impossible happens—if current trends don't change.

9 "We're doing projections, which are not forecasts or predictions," said Jennifer Day, author of the report. "If the trends continue, this is where our population could be."

10 The information is used by marketers, policymakers, educators and labor force experts to plan for the future.

11 When the Census Bureau made similar projections in 1987, it expected changes in the nation's immigration laws, combined with lower fertility rates, to cause slower population growth. But immigration did not slow, and the fertility rate of American women, particularly black women, has been rising since the late 1980s.

12 While the Census Bureau projects only population, race and age information, the America of 60 years from today is likely to be even more different than the America of 60 years ago, according to a variety of futurists.

Among the possibilities:

13 **• Race relations:** As America becomes more diverse, the melting pot will be tested once again.

14   If the early 20th century is any model, some experts believe that many of today's racial and ethnic distinctions might vanish.

15   When immigrants from Southern and Eastern Europe flocked to America between 1905 and 1914, they were considered so foreign that many maintained they would never assimilate.

16   "Even the ones from Northern Europe were branded as mentally defective, largely because they didn't know English, and there was a great deal of concern that they would not be able to adapt for democratic values," said Jeffrey Passel, a demographer at The Urban Institute.

17   Today, the descendants of these immigrants are simply classified as "white." And their marriage to someone of English descent would hardly be considered a "mixed" union.

18   By 2050, the same may be true of the second- and third-generation descendants of today's Mexican-Americans, or Chinese-Americans.

19   **• The family:** If the disintegration of the family continues, one futurist believes the family one day may not exist at all.

20   "A lot of people feel the family has served its purpose, if it ever really had one, and we no longer need the family," said Edward Cornish, president of the World Future Society.

21   More babies would be produced in laboratories. They might be raised by robots.

22   "Parents are notoriously weak in many areas of parenting, and under a carefully controlled system of robots and computers, we might have a much more peaceful society and even a much happier society," Mr. Cornish said.

23   **• The environment:** A growing American population could stress the environment, according to Susan Weber, executive director of Zero Population Growth.

24   Population growth in the United States is, in some ways, more troublesome than population growth in the rest of the world, because each American consumes so much more than people in other countries.

25   "It's not a formula for peace and well-being," Ms. Weber said. "It's a formula for strife."

26   Destruction of the world by nuclear war, though, is not the concern it once was.

27   "It looks like we're going to still be here," said Brad Strickland, a Gainesville College professor who writes fantasy and science fiction. "But I have a strong concern that we're facing a very great ecological upheaval in the next 40 or 50 years."

28   **• Influence of baby boomers:** As the bell curve of the baby boom moves toward its final flat line during the next 60 years, the generation may continue to have a strong influence on the society.

29   Gary Burtless, an economist at the Brookings Institution, guesses that Social Security and retirement benefits might not be awarded until some age past 65. Otherwise, the burden of so many retirees would be too great on the younger segment of the population.

30   "Wages aren't going to go up fast enough to make up for supporting the elderly," he said.

31   Mr. Burtless also wonders whether having a much older society will mean that America will be a more conservative place, less likely to embrace the kind of rapid social change that occurred in the 1960s.

32   "One of the reasons those attitudes changed so much was just that the population was so young," he said. "There's no doubt that the aging of the population is going to change the society in an important kind of way, but I'm not quite sure what it is."

33   **• Technology:** Computer technology will be so pervasive by 2050 that the average house may look something like the Starship Enterprise.

34   Cars probably will drive themselves.

Comprehension

True/False

Decide whether each statement is true or false according to the information in the article and the graphs. Then put T (true) or F (false) in the blank to the left of the question number. Explain why you answered "true" or "false" in the answer blanks that follow each question.

_____ 1. By 2050, the average person will expect to live six years longer than in 1990.

        _____

        _____

_____ 2. By 2050, blacks will no longer be the largest minority in the United States.

        _____

        _____

_____ 3. By 2050, whites will continue to constitute a majority of the U.S. population.

        _____

        _____

_____ 4. In regard to the increase in the Asian population, there is a discrepancy between what the graph shows and what the writer states.

        _____

        _____

_____ 5. By 2050, the baby boomers will be middle aged.

        _____

        _____

_____ 6. According to the writer, census experts predict that America will double
its population by 2050.

_____

_____

_____ 7. The Census Bureau's projections have always proved to be accurate.

_____

_____

_____ 8. By studying population trends, the Census Bureau can predict whether
there will be an improvement in race relations.

_____

_____

_____ 9. Some futurists predict that there will be an increase in marriages between persons of different races and ethnicity.

_____

_____

_____10. The president of the World Future Society **implies** that parents are to
blame for much of the unhappiness and unrest in American society.

_____

_____

_____11. The reader can **infer** that Susan Weber would be in favor of curbing the
birthrate in America.

_____

_____

Your Opinion: Discuss or Write

— What effect can different ethnic groups have on a society? If you come from an ethnically diverse society, use your country as an example.

— What effect can a growing elderly population have on a society? How are the elderly regarded in your country? As a burden on the young? As experienced and therefore wise?

Glossary

The numbers in front of the words indicate the paragraphs (in the reading) in which the words are found. Stressed syllables are underlined.

(2)	cater (v.)	to provide comfort and pleasure to
(2)	doddering (adj.)	shaky or trembling
(8)	trend (n.)	a general direction; tendency
(11)	fertility (n.)	ability to bear children
(12)	futurist (n.)	a person who forecasts future events
(15)	assimilate (v.)	to (cause to) become part of a nation in customs and attitudes
(19)	disintegration (n.)	breaking up
(22)	notorious (adj.)	publicly and generally known; widely and unfavorably known
(23)	stress (v.)	to cause harm to
(25)	strife (n.)	trouble between people; quarreling

6. Teach Your Children Well

(by Paul Gray, Time*)*

Preparing to Read

— Skim the following excerpt from an article in *Time* magazine. What do you think the article will be about?

— Think about your own experiences in learning the English language.

NOW READ THE ARTICLE THROUGH.

TEACH
Your Children Well

But what to teach the newest arrivals in what language
still vexes the nation's public schools

By PAUL GRAY

1 O N A CLOUDY WINTER afternoon, Florann Greenberg, a teacher at P.S. 14 in New York City, noticed that her first-grade class was growing fidgety. One girl, dropping all pretense of work, stared at the snow falling outside the schoolroom windows. Annoyed, Greenberg asked her, "Haven't you seen snow before?" The girl whispered, "No." Her classmates began shaking their heads. Then it dawned on Greenberg: *of course* these children had never seen snow; almost all were immigrants from Colombia and the Dominican Republic. Immediately, she changed the lesson plan. New topic: What is snow? How is it formed? How do you dress in the snow? What games do you play?

2 Such moments of cultural dissonance, followed by attempts to learn and teach from them, now take place daily in thousands of classrooms scattered across the U.S. The children of the new immigrants, often immigrants themselves, have been arriving at these classrooms in growing numbers, and more are on the way. They are placing unprecedented demands on teachers, administrators and already strained school systems. To a heartening degree, however, educators are responding with fresh, pragmatic methods of coping with these new demands.

3 Isolated numbers hint at the scope of the challenge:

• Total enrollment in U.S. public schools rose only 4.2% between 1986 and 1991, according to a 1993 Urban Institute study, while the number of students with little or no knowledge of English increased 50%, from 1.5 million to 2.3 million.

4 • In the Washington school system, students speak 127 languages and dialects; across the Potomac, in Fairfax County, Virginia, that figure is more than 100.

5 • In California public schools 1 out of 6 students was born outside the U.S., and 1 in 3 speaks a language other than English at home. The Los Angeles school system now absorbs 30,000 new immigrant children each year.

6 Such figures, startling as they are, have stirred little national attention, in part because the new immigrant families have not spread themselves uniformly across the country. A recent Rand Corp. study found that 78% of school-age immigrants who have been in the U.S. three years or less live in just five states: California, New York, Texas, Florida and Illinois. Like most statistics, this one can be misleading if it is taken to mean that the surge of immigrant students is solely a big-state, big-city concern. In absolute terms, even a small number of such students can profoundly affect the way a school district goes about its business.

7 In Garden City, Kansas (pop. 24,600), a boom in the meat-packing industry that began during the 1980s continues to attract aspiring workers, principally from Mexico and Southeast Asia. Now, of the 3,666 children in Garden City's elementary schools, roughly 700 require special help because of limited proficiency in English. Lowell, Massachusetts, was a fading city of 19th century textile mills until 1985, when the Federal Government chose it as a resettlement site for Southeast Asian families. This year, aided by federal and state grants, Lowell spent $5.9 million on bilingual education; courses are offered in Spanish, Khmer, Lao, Portuguese and Vietnamese. All communications between schools and parents are translated into five languages. At the Cary Reynolds elementary school in the Atlanta suburb of De Kalb County, Georgia, students from 25 foreign nations speak a medley of languages ranging from Mandarin to Farsi.

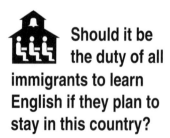

Should it be the duty of all immigrants to learn English if they plan to stay in this country?

YES 96%   NO 4%

From a telephone poll of 1,108 adult Americans taken for TIME/CNN on Sept. 8-9 by Yankelovich Partners Inc. Sampling error is ±3%.

8   In practice, many teachers have begun turning the problems of ethnic diversity in their classrooms to educational advantage. Most elementary schools in Garden City celebrate different national holidays, including Mexican Independence Day, the Laotian New Year and Vietnam's Tet. Last year a class at New York City's P.S. 189, which is roughly one-third Haitian, performed a class project about Jean-Jacques Dessalines, the slave who freed Haiti from France. The exercise was consistent with both Haitian cultural traditions and the school's emphasis on maintaining harmony and diversity.

9   But the nation's school systems are not being swept by the kind of wholesale changes that traditionalists feared would result from such programs as New York City's controversial "Children of the Rainbow" curriculum and Portland, Oregon's baseline essays, which aim to reduce the perceived Eurocentric bias of U.S. education. The ideological debate about multicultural education, brewing for years on college campuses, does not seem to have leached into primary and secondary schools, where math, science, geography, etc., are still regarded as important. Nonetheless, vexing but essential questions prevail: How are students who know no English to be taught? Must they, in the process, sacrifice their ethnic or cultural heritage?

    Surprisingly, most educators who work with the new immigrants believe competence in English and the maintenance of cultural identity are compatible goals. "I believe in language and cultural pride," says Martin Gross, a New York City elementary school principal, "but let's not forget the fact that these kids are in America. I think we should respect different cultures but not become factionalized." Claudia Hammock, a teacher at the Cary Reynolds school, agrees: "We do try to keep their native customs and try to show them we want them to remember. But we also want them to learn to function in an English-speaking world."

    To reach that goal, teachers and administrators have, over several years of trial and error, evolved two different methods. In one, students are plunged immediately into intensive E.S.L. (English as a Second Language) instruction; the idea is to bring them up to the proficiency of native speakers at their grade level and get them into mainstream classes as quickly as possible. The other, bilingual, approach allows students to take courses such as math and history in their own language while devoting a certain amount of time each day to learning English. Once the new language has been mastered, the students can translate and build upon their earlier, non-English instruction.

12   Both techniques have proved appealing to students. Carol Ovndo, 12, arrived in Fairfax County from Guatemala three years ago without knowing a word of English. Her immersion in all-English courses rapidly enabled her to become a proficient speaker and reader. "It was scary," she recalls. "But my teacher showed me pictures, and my friends helped, and sometimes we just all acted things out." At the Bell Multi-Cultural High School in Washington, Nguyen Nguyen, 15, who arrived from Vietnam a year ago, takes courses in both his native language and English. "I have to understand in Vietnamese first," he says, "so I can translate it into English. I learn best this way."

13   Both techniques have their drawbacks. English-only works better for younger students but can prove too rigorous for older children, who may grow frustrated and disinterested in school as a result. Children who live in families and communities where a foreign language is spoken often take so long to master English that they lack basic factual knowledge once they enter mainstream courses.

14   Most teachers now prefer the bilingual method. Says Winnie Porter, a bilingual teacher at the Cesar Chavez Elementary School in San Francisco: "It's very simple. You teach children in the language they think in; then they understand the concepts. Once they understand the concepts, they can transfer these skills to a second language. I know it works. I've been doing it for 10 years and see the results." But many communities cannot afford or attract qualified bilingual teachers in all— or any—of the subjects students may need. Says Gloria McDonell, director of the Fairfax County E.S.L. program: "We don't teach bilingual education because it's impractical. It's hard to find someone who can teach math in Korean."

Comprehension

True/False

Decide whether each statement is true or false according to the information in the article. Then put T (true) or F (false) in the blank to the left of the question number. Explain any "false" answers in the answer blanks that follow each question.

_____ 1. The number of children who speak little or no English has caused the total enrollment in the public schools in the United States to increase by 50 percent.

\
_____

\
_____

_____ 2. The reader can **infer** that some immigrants settle in small towns so that their children will be given a bilingual education.

\
_____

\
_____

_____ 3. In the bilingual approach to educating immigrant children, there is no need for ESL instruction since all courses are offered in the children's native languages.

\
_____

\
_____

_____ 4. The goal of both the English-only method and the bilingual method of teaching English is to enter the immigrant children into regular classes as soon as possible.

_____

_____

_____ 5. The reader can **infer** that in order to function in an English-speaking society, children must be taught never to forget their cultural heritage.

_____

_____

_____ 6. The word *factionalized* in paragraph 10 means being interested in one's own group to the exclusion of others.

_____

_____

_____ 7. According to the poll cited in this article, the American public is indifferent to what language or languages Americans speak.

_____

_____

Questions and Discussion (Written or Oral)

1. In your own words, briefly explain the difference between the bilingual method and the English-only method of teaching English to immigrant children. Which do you think is the better method and why?

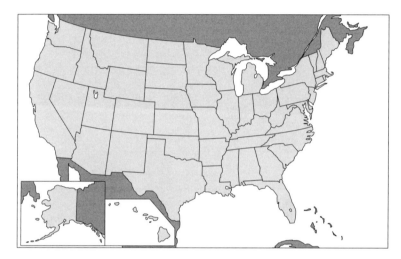

2. Why do you think the five states mentioned in paragraph 6 would have 78 percent of the school-age immigrants who have been in the United States three years or less? (Consult a map of the United States.)

3. You know the meaning of *bilingual*. Guess the meanings of *multilingual* and *monolingual*.

4. Is English the official language of the United States? Do you think it "should be the duty of all immigrants to learn English if they plan to stay in this country"? Explain your answer.

Vocabulary Study

Guessing the Meanings of Words from Context

Try to guess the meanings of the following words from their context. (The numbers in parentheses are the numbers of the reading paragraphs in which these words occur.) Underline the words, phrases, or sentences in the reading that helped you guess the meanings. You may work with a partner.

(2)   pragmatic* (adj.): _____

(6)   uniformly (adv.): _____

(7)   proficiency (n.): _____

(11) mainstream (adj.): _____

(13) drawback (n.): _____

Glossary

The numbers in front of the words indicate the paragraphs (in the reading) in which the words are found. Stressed syllables are underlined.

(1)	fidgety (adj.)	restless
(2)	dissonance (n.)	difference; contrast
(3)	scope (n.)	extent
(10)	compatible (adj.)	able to exist together
(12)	immersion (n.)	deep involvement
(14)	concept (n.)	idea

---

*Stressed syllables are underlined.

Review: Vocabulary

Fill in each blank in the following sentences with the appropriate word from the
list. Use the correct tenses of the verbs.

assimilate	fringe	proficient
compatible	mainstream	proliferate
disintegration	milestone	strife
drawback	notorious	vex
fidgety	overwhelming	

1. He is a _____ liar; no one believes anything he says.

2. Because we stood on the _____ of the crowd, we were not able to hear

    everything the president said.

3. The invention of television was a _____ in

    communications.

4. As soon as Ann found that she and her new boss were not _____, she

    quit her job.

5. Being late to class is sure to _____ our teacher.

6. One _____ of living in the suburbs is having to travel a long distance

    to get to one's job.

7. Unless there is more gun control, the sales of guns will _____.

8. An _____ majority of voters would reelect a president who kept his

    promise to reduce taxes.

9. Young children become _____ when they have to sit quietly for any

    length of time.

10. Becoming _____ in any foreign language is no easy task.

11. The United States has _____ immigrants from many countries.

12. Armed _____ has resulted in thousands of deaths in the former

    Yugoslavia.

13. The _____ of relations between the two countries signaled that war was

    imminent.

14. The goal of educators is to get immigrant children into _____ classes

    as soon as possible.

7.   What Is a Family?

(by Bernard Gavzer, Parade*)*

Preparing to Read

Discuss the following questions as they relate to your country.

— Is there a high rate of divorce?

— Do men and women live together before marriage?

— Are there many children born out of wedlock?

— Do mothers work outside the home?

— Do many people live alone?

Writing before You Read

How would you define a strong, stable family? Write your definition in one or two paragraphs.

NOW READ THE ARTICLE THROUGH.

*It has become one of the critical questions
for the nation's future:*

What Is
A Family?

1 THE QUESTION OF values—what they are and who has them—was one of the most emotional issues of the recent election. Now that the dust has settled, PARADE decided to take another look at a subject almost all agree will have a tremendous impact on America's future.

2 The definition of family in America has been changing radically in the last few decades (see box, "The American Family"). For one thing, the traditional family—two parents, a father who works and a mother who raises her two or three children at home—is waning, with a high divorce rate (nearly one in two marriages fails) battering it even further. At the same time, one-parent families are becoming more common, whether by choice or circumstance.

3 We also are seeing more of those domestic set-ups that some say are families and that others adamantly maintain aren't. Who is right? What is a "family" anyway? And what values should a family, any family, strive for?

4 Talk of the demise of the American family is not new. "For more than 100 years—with the exception of the baby boom," says Larry Bumpass, a University of Wisconsin demographer, "Western society has taken a course of increased emphasis on the individual and his own interests and well-being, and decreased emphasis on the family and family obligations." Yet there is a widespread feeling today that something is wrong. Experts cite grim statistics on divorce, teenage pregnancy, incest, single parents, unwed couples and abandonment.

5 There is no single type of family that can be solely identified with these problems. Families of wealth, power and education are no more immune from disruption than those of poverty. In recent years, for example, we have been treated to confessional books by the children of Ronald and Nancy Reagan, Joan Crawford, Lana Turner and Bing Crosby.* They revealed lives of desperation and dysfunction.

6 Strong families, however, have certain things in common: They are built out of two powerful commitments, say the experts. These are to nurture and protect the young while preparing them to join society; and to protect and support the well-being of the elderly.

7 These two goals are prized among people who differ in race, religion, wealth, heritage and culture. And they are shared by people whose lifestyles are both traditional and nontraditional, says Thomas F.

Coleman, director of the nonprofit Spectrum Institute's Family Diversity Project in Los Angeles.

8 A strong family often starts with a strong marriage. Although marriage is no guarantee of a positive family environment, it is the first step to a strong family.

9 What makes for a strong marriage? "There are two key components," explains Dr. Krister Stendahl, a theologian and professor of Christian studies at

BY BERNARD GAVZER

*Motion picture actors of the 1940s and 1950s. Ronald Reagan was later president of the United States (1981–89).

Brandeis University. "One is fidelity—a faithfulness and loyalty between man and wife. The other is mutuality— being equal, not using one another."

10 Don Cone, 71, and his wife, Doris, 70, of Baywood Park, Calif., may typify such a marriage in its most traditional sense. The Cones, who've been married for 50 years, first appeared in PARADE in 1955 as a typical middle-class couple with three children. Two of their children are married and have children of their own; one son is a retired Navy man. Don Cone sacrificed a possible career at the top tier in the corporate world to build a strong family.

11 "It was clear in my company that if you were going to get ahead, you had to give your life to the company," says Cone, who was an engineer engaged in developing color TV. "But I put the Presbyterian Church and my work with the Boy Scouts and my family ahead of everything else."

12 Patricia Conway, 41, a teacher in Portland, Oregon, and James Brunkow, 42, a chimney sweep, are not married. But they've been together for 11 years and have four children: Matthew, 10; Jacy, 8; Ian, 6; and Kelsey Rose, 3. Their family is the center of their life. Their huge kitchen table is crowded with children doing homework or with everyone diving into huge meals. The family spends much time together.

13 Yet Conway and Brunkow are not legally recognized as a family. The Census Bureau defines a "family" as those related by blood, marriage or adoption. Failing to meet that criteria, unwed couples can run into complications, ranging from getting health insurance to trying to file joint income-tax returns.

14 "Being married is not the issue," says Brunkow. "The commitment I make to Patricia and the kids is one I make freely. We are choosing to live in this fashion. Because we do it doesn't mean that we should be denied any of the benefits that normally exist between people who are married."

15 Dmitri Belser, 34, and Tom White, 37, who are homosexuals, call themselves a family too. Though the pair have taken upon themselves the responsibilities of a marriage and family, they also are unable to get the benefits of one, because the law does not recognize such unions as "marriages."

16 "We *are* a family," insists Belser. "We have two sons, Elliott, 7, and Sabastian, 3. The adoption decree names us both as parents, acknowledging the relationship. But the state won't recognize us as a couple, even though everything we have is held in common."

17 They were able to adopt their sons through networking. "We knew Elliott's mother from when she was in her second month, and we went through the

A Snapshot of the American Family, 1992

THE CENSUS BUREAU HAS PUT together a statistical profile of the different kinds of households in America, based on a comparison of data from 1970 to 1991. Here are some of the notable changes:
• The two largest family groups are what the Census Bureau describes as "married couples without children at home" and "married couples with at least one child under 18 living at home." Since 1970, the first group has remained fairly constant, at about 30% of the population; the latter, however, has shrunk. In 1970, such families made up 40% of all households; today, they account for just 26%.
• The number of single-parent families in America has increased drastically since 1970, when there were 3.8 million of them, or 12.9% of all the families with children. In 1991, there were 10.1 million, or 29% of all families with children. Mothers head almost 90% of the single-parent families in this country.
• In 1970, nearly 400,000 babies were born to single mothers, or 11% of all births in the country. More than a million such babies were born to

unwed mothers in 1989 (the most recent year for which figures are available), or 27% of all births.
•The number of unmarried couples in the country swelled from 523,000 in 1970 to 3 million in 1991. Larry Bumpass, a demographer at the University of Wisconsin, says 40% of these couples have children.
•In 1991, same-sex households accounted for 2% of all families—about the same as in 1970. There were children in 5% of these households.
•The number of people living alone has increased dramatically, from 20% of all households in 1970 to 30% today. The Census Bureau lists such households as "nonfamilies." This label applies to households with one individual—or more, if the residents are not related.

One reason for the 10% increase in "nonfamilies" is the growing number of elderly Americans, particularly women over the age of 75. Also contributing is the number of college-aged youths who share apartments, individuals who live alone while they decide to delay or forgo marriage and those who are between marriages.

entire pregnancy and delivery with her," says Belser. "We got Sabastian when he was 5 months old."

18 While, for some, a two-father household may seem like an extreme interpretation of "family," other changes in American society in the last few decades have been affecting the beliefs many Americans grew up with.

19 Perhaps most powerful is the change in women's roles: This has affected thinking about how a woman should live her life and opened discussion about what a child needs from a parent—and from which parent.

20 The dual-income family is one in which both parents are working and probably spending less time with their kids. In 1960, just 20% of mothers with children under 6 were in the labor force; by last year, 58% of such women were working, mostly full-time.

21 "Increasingly, families rely on the woman's earnings," says Rep. Pat Schroeder (D., Colo.), who heads the House Select Committee on Children, Youth and Families. "That income can make a critical difference, enabling them to own a home, send a child to college or, in an increasing number of families, to just get by."

22 "The important thing for working parents," says Dr. Martha Welch, a child psychiatrist, "is to convey to their children that the kids are their top priority."

23 But it isn't always that simple. Jill Lawrence, an Associated Press writer, and her husband, John Martin, managing editor of *Governing* magazine, have had to figure out how to juggle the interests and needs of their sons—Alex, 7, and Greg, 3—against the demands of their jobs and their commitment to their careers. They've arranged work schedules so that they are home in time to have meals with the boys and read to them or tell stories before going to bed.

24 "As well as we do, money is still a problem," says Lawrence. "Even if it wasn't, I'd want to work. I love being a mother, but I also love what I do."

25 Most single mothers have no choice: They must work to support their families. But while such families can be strong and stable, sharing the same goals for their kids as two-parent families, they are particularly at risk.

26 One in four babies is now born to an unwed mother (compared to one in 10 in 1970), and about half of all children today are expected to spend some part of their childhood in a single-parent family. The link between poverty and single mothers is overwhelming. In 1990, 45% of all female-headed households with children aged 18 or younger fell below the poverty line, compared to just 8% of two-parent families.

27 Statistics show how quickly a broken family pushes women and children into poverty. One rea-

son is nonpayment of child support. Of the 5 million women eligible for such support, only half reported receiving full payment, according to a 1990 Census Bureau study. To change that situation, pressure is building around the country to get divorced fathers to promptly and steadily pay alimony and child support. Some experts say it also might be time to make it more difficult to get divorces—especially in cases involving children. In addition, a variety of programs and organizations are committed to helping families at risk.

28 For single mothers, a workplace sensitive to the needs of parents is important. "I found working mothers who say that they would never call in and tell the boss they had a sick child," says Representative Schroeder. "Instead, they would say their car had a radiator leak, and the boss could understand that."

29 Barbara Reisman, director of the Child Care Action Campaign, says: "There are 5600 companies that provide some form of child-care benefit—such as helping to find such care, pay for it or provide it directly. There also are other companies that are family-friendly." This means they may offer flex time, parental leave and other forms of child care. But, most of all, they recognize the value of enabling employees to balance family and work responsibilities.

30 Beth Munger, 30, of Portland, Ore., is a young married mother who resolved the work/day care/home-leave problem by finding a job that lets the children (Paul Eugene, 6, who attends kindergarten for half a day; Jeffrey, 4; and James, 2) stay with her most of the time. She works at Kids At Heart, a shop with environmentally attuned toys and games. "They can show other kids how things work," says Beth. "I love having them with me."

31 Linda Walker has been a single mother for 11 years. Her husband left when she was pregnant. For two years, she lived in a shelter for the homeless in Chicago with her four children and two young relatives who are her dependents. "Being on public assistance shamed me," she says. "I resented the fact I didn't have the education that helps a person be independent."

32 Things changed for the better in October 1991, when she moved into subsidized housing. She began working as a counselor for the homeless last July. Each day, Walker delivers the message of the need for education to her children—and her daughter, Lenora, seems to have received it. At age 13, she was recognized by the Chicago Department of Education as a gifted child.

33 "I blanket them with love, but that doesn't do away with discipline," says Walker. "We are a family."

Comprehension

Defining "Family"

How does the United States Census Bureau define a "family"?

According to this definition, which of the following would be considered "nonfamilies"? Circle the appropriate numbers.

1. household: single father and child
2. household: elderly woman and companion/housekeeper
3. household: unmarried couple living as husband and wife
4. household: single mother and adopted child
5. household: one individual
6. household: married couple and adult children

True/False

Decide whether each statement is true or false according to the information in the article. Then put T (true) or F (false) in the blank to the left of the question number.

_____ 1. "Single mothers" can refer to either unwed or divorced mothers.

_____ 2. The reader can **infer** that in the state in which Belser and White live, it is not illegal for a homo-sexual couple to adopt a child.

_____ 3. Nearly 50 percent of all marriages in the United States fail.

_____ 4. About half of all children in the United States are born to unwed mothers.

_____ 5. One can **infer** from paragraph 28 that "the boss" is most likely a man. Explain your answer ("true" or "false") in the answer blanks.

_____

_____

_____ 6. A family-friendly company means that the bosses and their employees socialize outside the workplace.

_____ 7. In 1960, 20 percent of mothers with children under 6 were working outside the home; by 1991, the number had almost tripled.

_____ 8. The reader can **infer** that many fathers are not devoted to their children. Explain your answer ("true" or "false") in the answer blanks.

_____

_____

_____ 9. The writer gives several reasons for the increase in the number of unwed mothers.

Comprehension

Questions and Discussion (Written or Oral)

Answer the following questions based on the information in the article.

1. Why has there been an increase in one-parent families in the United States? Discuss the difficulties that result from the single-parent family. Why do you think mothers head almost 90 percent of the single-parent families?

2. Has the changing role of women had both a positive and a negative effect on the American family? Explain your answer.

3. According to the article, are there any solutions for the problems working mothers face? If so, what are they?

4. Why do Patricia Conway and James Brunkow, although unmarried, believe that they meet the criteria of a strong family? Do you agree? Why or why not? Why do you think these two people remain unmarried?

Your Opinion: Discuss or Write

— How do you feel about the nontraditional "families" described in the article? Has the definition of family also changed in your country in the last few decades? Explain your answer.

— What do you think are the reasons for the high rate of divorce and the increase in out-of-wedlock births in the United States? What do you think can be done to stop the decline of the traditional American family?

Vocabulary Study

Guessing the Meanings of Words from Context

Following are some excerpts from the reading selection. Try to guess the meaning of each circled word or phrase by studying the underlined words and phrases. You may want to work with a partner.

1. "The <u>definition</u> of <u>family</u> in <u>America</u> has been <u>changing</u> (radically) in the last few decades. . . . the <u>traditional</u> <u>family</u> . . . is (waning,) with a <u>high divorce rate</u> . . . . <u>one-parent families</u> are becoming <u>more common</u>. . . .
   Talk of the (demise) of the <u>American family</u> is not new. . . . Experts cite (grim) <u>statistics</u> on <u>divorce, teenage pregnancy, incest, single parents, unwed couples</u> and <u>abandonment</u>." (pars. 2,4)

   <u>rad</u>ically* (adv.): _____

   wane (v.): _____

   de<u>mise</u> (n.): _____

   grim (adj.): _____

2. "What makes for a strong marriage? . . . 'One [component] is (fidelity) — a faithfulness and loyalty between man and wife. The other is (mutuality) — being equal, not using one another.'" (par. 9)

   fi<u>del</u>ity (n.): _____

   mutu<u>al</u>ity (n.): _____

   Note: Fidelity and mutuality are defined for you. (Refer to p. 8, no. 2.)

3. "The (dual-income family) is one in which both parents are working . . . ." (par. 20)

   <u>dual</u>-<u>in</u>come family (adj.; n.): _____

   Note: The writer defines this phrase.

---

*Stressed syllables of the circled words are underlined.

4. "The(link)between <u>poverty</u> and <u>single mothers</u> is(overwhelming.)In 1990, <u>45%</u> of all <u>female-headed households</u> with <u>children aged 18</u> or <u>younger</u> fell <u>below</u> the <u>poverty</u> line, compared to just <u>8%</u> of <u>two-parent families</u>." (par. 26)

    link (n.): _____

    overwhelming (adj.): _____

5. "... pressure is building around the country to get <u>divorced fathers</u> to promptly and steadily pay(alimony)and <u>child support</u>." (par. 27)

    <u>alimony</u> (n.): _____

Paraphrasing

Paraphrasing is restating a phrase, a sentence, or sentences *in your own words* in order to more easily understand difficult reading material.

Paraphrase the following passages from the article on the American family. First, try to guess the meanings of unfamiliar words from context. (As a last resort,* consult your English/English dictionary.) Then, restate the passage *in your own words.* Work with a partner.

1. "Families of wealth, power and education are no more immune from disruption than those of poverty." (par. 5)
    Example: The breakup of the family can occur among the rich, powerful, and educated as well as among the poor.

2. "'The important thing for working parents,' says Dr. Martha Welch, a child psychiatrist, 'is to convey to their children that the kids are their top priority.'" (par. 22)

    _____

    _____

3. "Jill Lawrence . . . and her husband, John Martin, . . . have had to figure out how to juggle the interests and needs of their sons — Alex, 7, and Greg, 3 — against the demands of their jobs and their commitment to their careers." (par. 23)

    _____

    _____

---

*As a last resort = if everything else fails

4. "Most single mothers have no choice: They must work to support their families. But while such families can be strong and stable, sharing the same goals for their kids as two-parent families, they are particularly at risk." (par. 25)

_____

_____

5. "'I blanket them with love, but that doesn't do away with discipline,' says Walker." (par. 33)

_____

_____

Glossary

The numbers in front of the words indicate the paragraphs (in the reading) in which the words are found. Stressed syllables are underlined.

(1)	values (n.)	standards; people's ideas about the worth of certain qualities
(2)	batter (v.)	ruin, destroy
(3)	setup (n.)	an arrangement
(4)	incest (n.)	a sexual relationship between close relatives in a family, as between brother and sister
(5)	dysfunction (n.)	instability
(6)	commitment (n.)	a pledge or promise; obligation
(15)	homosexual (n.)	a person sexually attracted to people of the same sex
(17)	networking (n.)	sharing information and services among individuals and groups having a common interest
(29)	flex time (n.)	an arrangement by which employees may set their own work schedules, as starting and finishing hours

8. Mothers Are Always Special

(by Celestine Sibley)

Preparing to Read

The following true story is from the book *Mothers Are Always Special,* a collection of stories about mothers by Celestine Sibley. Ms. Sibley, an award-winning journalist and columnist for the *Atlanta Constitution,* is one of the South's most popular writers.

Before you read this *feel-good* story, look up the word *miracle* in your English/English dictionary. *Do you believe in miracles?*

NOW READ THE ARTICLE THROUGH.

Mothers Are Always Special

Celestine Sibley

1   **THE DECISIONS INVOLVED** in being a mother are sometimes so frightening you wonder how any woman has the courage to make them. The most courageous woman I ever saw was a big-eyed country girl named Montell Purcell. She took the responsibility of a life-and-death or, as the newspaper called it at the time, death-or-blindness decision on herself.

2   It was New Year's Eve 1951 when I first heard of the Purcells. A friend whose husband was in the hospital called and told me that while she was waiting out her husband's operation she got to talking to a woman whose five-year-old daughter was in the hospital to have her eyes checked.

3   "That little girl, that *baby*, has cancer!" cried my friend. "The doctor just told the mother she will have to have her eyes removed or she will die!"

4   It was what used to be known as a human-interest story and I didn't have much heart for it. It was the holiday season and nobody wants to read—or to write— sad stories. But after a day or two my conscience hurt me and I went looking for the Purcells and their little girl.

5   They had left the private infirmary where they had received the death-or-blindness diagnosis and gone to the city-county charity hospital, Grady, in the hope of finding better news. I found them in the children's ward there—Frank, the father, a quiet, country-reared man of forty, who had recently been laid off* by a small-town textile mill, and his wife, Montell, thirty-three. They sat beside the bed of a frisky, beautiful little girl named Carolyn, who had bright brown eyes and hair to match curling around a piquant face and pulled into a pigtail in the back.

6   They told me the story.

7   Carolyn was their only child and although they had to work hard for everything they had, at Christmastime they took special pleasure in buying their little girl everything they dreamed she would like. Before Frank was laid off at the mill Montell had bought and put away Carolyn's Christmas toys and they both felt relieved and happy that the specter of unemployment wouldn't mar Christmas morning at their house. One of the presents Montell was happiest over and the one that cost the most was a new tri-cycle. Carolyn had seen tricycles and had talked of nothing else in all the weeks leading up to Christmas.

8   When Christmas morning dawned the child was out of bed before her father could get up and build a fire. She went straight for the Christmas tree and, stumbling a little (her mother thought from excitement), she found the doll. She looked around and at and over the new tricycle—without seeing it.

9   "She didn't know it was there," her mother said chokily. "The tricycle she wanted so bad."

10 As the morning passed and Carolyn gradually discovered and played with her toys, Frank and Montell, looking at each other fearfully, began to realize that their little girl, the child with the bright, beautiful eyes, couldn't see.

11 They had little money and they knew almost nothing about getting around Atlanta, although they had grown up and lived all their adult lives less than fifty miles from the city limits. But they were undaunted in their determination to find the best medical help for Carolyn. I found out later the reason they acted so swiftly was that their first child, a little girl named Mary Marjorie, had died without medical attention of what the father called "a kind of mystery disease" ten years before Carolyn was born. The day after Christmas they took Carolyn to a country doctor who recommended a city specialist and arranged an appointment for them.

12 It was at the ear-eyes-nose-throat infirmary that they learned for the first time that Carolyn's trouble was not simple nearsightedness which could be corrected by glasses but something which could cost her life. The name the doctor gave it was glioma.

---

*lay off: to dismiss a worker, esp. temporarily

13   Hoping against hope that the doctor was mistaken, they had come to Grady, the hospital where most Atlanta doctors teach or serve on the staff as consultants. When I found them, Carolyn was being given a series of tests and was being examined by five or six of the city's other leading eye specialists.

14   They had been in the hospital for two or three days when the results of a clinic held by the entire staff on ophthalmology were made known. A group of reporters had gathered and we stood in the hall with Montell and her parents when an intern brought up the report, a written diagnosis, and read it to them. It said, in effect, that the child did indeed have glioma, that she would have to lose one eye immediately and the other one probably very soon.

15   There hadn't been much real hope in the Purcells and in Montell's family, the Dinsmores. They were resigned to the operation. Frank, looking stricken, saw no other course.

16   Surprisingly, when we all turned to Montell, her answer was a low-voiced, "No."

17   A delay, the young intern explained patiently, might be dangerous.

18   "No," said Montell again. "We'll wait."

19   That night she and Frank took Carolyn and, against the doctors' advice, left the hospital. They went to the home of some relatives who ran a truck stop on a four-lane highway twenty miles north of Atlanta. I saw them almost daily and I felt close enough to Montell to ask her how she dared to wait. She was a woman of little education and, of course, no medical skill. How dare she pit her knowledge against the best medical opinion available in the hospitals and medical schools of our town?

20   It was then she told me about Mary Marjorie.

21   She and Frank were very young and very poor when Mary Marjorie was born. They lived on a farm in one of the mountain counties, miles from the nearest doctor and with no car. One day the little girl got sick. All day long Montell nursed her, using such home remedies as she knew about, and steadily the child grew worse.

22   Frank started walking for help and along about dusk came back home with a borrowed truck. They wrapped Mary Marjorie up and started to the nearest doctor. The child died on the way.

23   "I know the Lord don't always answer you the way you want Him to," Montell said, "but I believe He answers you. All day long I prayed that He would make my baby well. He didn't answer my prayer that way but I felt He had a purpose and when the answer come I could take it. I'm praying now and I got to wait."

24   While Montell waited, people all over the world seemed stirred by the story. Soldiers in Korea wrote her, expressing sympathy and encouragement. Convicts in prisons offered their eyes. Some people urged the operation, some warned her against it. The great Helen Keller wrote and told her not to be afraid, blindness was not so bad, a child could give up her eyes and still have a good life. Advice poured in from every corner of the world. Faith healers came and marched and prayed and sang in the yard. Sightseers came just to look at the child and her parents.

25   And through it all, Montell, a real gentlewoman, held up her head and smiled and thanked people. And waited.

26   After about a week, Fred Cannon, head of the local Shrine Horse Patrol, called me and said he had been reading the stories about Carolyn and he and his fellow Shriners* were deeply concerned. They had no doubt that the child should have the operation but they understood the mother's reluctance and they felt that another diagnosis from a high-placed source would help her decide. Would I ask her if she would take the child to the Mayo Clinic if I would go with her and the Shriners would pay the expense of the trip?

27   Both Frank and Montell were overwhelmed by the offer. I could see in Montell's white face the hungry hope that this was "the answer."

28   Gifts for the child came pouring in. "Papa Sunshine," a Jewish immigrant who ran a department store in a poor section of town, outfitted her with new clothes and a warm coat with a hat that had earmuffs for the cold Minnesota weather. There were toys and gifts of money and a big crowd gathered at the airport to see us off on a gray January day.

29   Carolyn was bouncy and bright-eyed, and Montell, although tired and pale, smiled a lot. And I privately worried that the child might die on the trip.

30   Wherever the plane stopped—and they were making more stops in 1951—people came out to greet Carolyn and to give her presents or to shout advice to her mother. Not once did Montell plead weariness or fail to smile and express her gratitude. It was night when we landed in

*Shriners: an organization that is dedicated to health programs, charitable works, and so forth.

Rochester and although the Shriners, wearing their cheery red fezzes, came out to meet us and to take us to the hotel adjoining the big clinic, it did seem a foreign land to all three of us. All that snow and ice, that unbroken, unrelenting whiteness.

31   The next day we learned that such examinations as Carolyn's take time and it might be several days before they could begin hers. In the meantime, we were to wait. Having a job and children of my own to worry about, I started making arrangements to turn Montell and Carolyn over to the hospital social service people when I saw Montell's courage falter a little. She had been so brave and so strong but she couldn't bear to be left alone now.

32   The social workers saw it too, and suddenly, miraculously, somebody stamped Carolyn's case "Emergency" and the next morning at daybreak she began her trip through that vast clinic.

33   All day long the child and her mother went from test to test, from examination to examination. I was waiting for them at dusk in a little room on the ground floor of the clinic. The lights had not been turned on but there was a strange, silvery twilight reflected from the snow outside. I stood at the window looking at the whiteness and the roof line of a little church strung with icicles.

34   Montell came in quietly. Carolyn, exhausted from the day's ordeal, was asleep in her mother's arms. Montell held in her hand a piece of paper on which somebody had written the verdict.

35   "Would you read it for me?" she asked.

36   I took the paper to the window and read. The child did not have cancer, she did not need to lose her eyes. The difficulty she had was caused by a nutritional deficiency. She could go home and be treated in Atlanta.

37   I looked up and Montell was looking out the window at the little church, with tears streaming down her cheeks.

38   "Thank you, Lord," she whispered. "I knowed You'd tell me."

39   Some people believe in miracles. I'm not sure that I do but Montell Purcell does. She said later, "You know all them doctors couldn't have been wrong. The Lord worked a miracle, He did."

40   If miracles exist, a stubborn, believing mother waited one out for Carolyn. Today Carolyn is a beautiful young married woman with a three-year-old daughter, Stephanie. Frank died in September 1968 and Montell now spends a lot of time with Carolyn and her family and smiles her warm, serene smile when friends remark that Carolyn's eyes are her prettiest feature.

41   "Did you know," she murmurs with a touch of awe, "she has twenty-twenty vision?"

Comprehension

Chronological Order

Put the following events from the reading into the order in which they occurred by writing the correct numbers in the answer blanks.

_____ The young mother wanted to wait.

_____ A private infirmary in Atlanta told the Purcells that their young daughter had cancer and would die unless her eyes were removed.

_____ Montell believed that God was responsible for the miracle that saved her daughter's eyesight.

_____ Carolyn and her parents went to the home of some relatives 20 miles north of Atlanta.

_____ The diagnosis was that she had no cancer but rather a nutritional deficiency.

_____ When Carolyn Purcell failed to notice her new tricycle on Christmas morning, her parents realized she couldn't see.

_____ Grady Hospital, a charity hospital in Atlanta, confirmed the diagnosis of cancer and recommended that one eye be removed immediately.

_____ "Papa Sunshine" gave the little girl new clothes and a warm coat to wear in Minnesota.

_____ Carolyn's case was stamped "Emergency," and she didn't have to wait several days to be examined at the Mayo Clinic.

_____ The Shriners offered to pay the expense of a trip to the Mayo Clinic in Minnesota in order to get another opinion.

_____ People from all over the world wrote the Purcells to express their sympathy and encouragement.

_____ Montell spends a lot of time with her daughter and granddaughter.

True/False

Decide whether each statement is true or false according to the information in the article. Then put T (true) or F (false) in the blank to the left of the question number.

_____ 1. Celestine Sibley and the Purcells had known each other long before the events in this story took place.

_____ 2. Montell's faith in God had been shaken after her first child died.

_____ 3. Unlike his wife, Frank Purcell was in favor of the operation on Carolyn's eye.

_____ 4. The doctors at the Mayo Clinic told Celestine Sibley the good news about Carolyn.

_____ 5. The reader can **infer** that an ophthalmologist is a doctor who specializes in the treatment of diseases of the eye.

_____ 6. The reader can **infer** that twenty-twenty vision is normal vision.

Comprehension

Questions and Discussion (Written or Oral)

Answer the following questions.

1. Ms. Sibley evidently thought that Montell Purcell was "special." Do you agree? Why or why not? If you had been in Montell's shoes,* what would your decision have been? Explain your answer.

2. Explain in your own words the reason for Carolyn's blindness. Was she cured? How does the reader know? How old would Carolyn be today?

3. Ms. Sibley writes that Montell "was a woman of little education." Can the reader **infer** from Montell's use of English that she was not well educated? If so, point out the evidence in the reading.

4. Why do you think the Shriners asked Ms. Sibley to accompany the Purcells to the Mayo Clinic?

5. There are several examples of *kindness* in this story. What are they? Do you think people are basically kind?

---

*in someone's shoes: in someone's situation

6. Do you agree with Montell that "the Lord worked a miracle. . . ."? Explain your answer.

7. Do you think there is a lesson to be learned from this story? Explain your answer.

9. The Modern Family

(by Beth B. Hess, Elizabeth W. Markson, and Peter J. Stein)

Preparing to Read

Reading Textbook Material

The following excerpt is from a chapter in a sociology textbook. When you want to *remember textbook information,* use the SQ3R method.

1. **Survey**. Read the title, the section headings, the marginal notes the author has provided, and the words in **boldface** and *italics*.

2. **Question**.* Before reading each section of the chapter, you will want to formulate some questions that you think the section will answer. Base your questions on the headings, the marginal notes, and the words in **boldface** and *italics*.

3. **Read**. Now read each section, keeping your questions in mind. *Underline the main ideas and the important supporting details.*

4. **Recite**. After reading each section of the text, *jot down from memory* the main points you have learned. These are your notes.

5. **Review**. When you have finished the entire reading, review your notes.

FOLLOWING THESE FIVE STEPS, READ THE ARTICLE AND STUDY FOR THE PRACTICE TEST (P. 92) ON "THE MODERN FAMILY."

---

*Your teacher will help you with this step.

THE MODERN FAMILY

Mate Selection in Modern Societies

If romantic love is the only legitimate reason for choosing a marriage partner, then people must be free to make their own choices. Parents can no longer arrange marriages for their children, although they can influence such choices directly (by signs of approval or disapproval) and indirectly (by moving to a certain part of town or joining a particular church). But in a modern society the burden of choice rests with the young people themselves, and each generation of youth has elaborated a set of norms and behaviors—dating rituals—to help them select a mate (Bailey, 1988).

Although dating rituals change over time in response to other changes in the society, the general pattern begins with a form of group dating where sets of boys and girls, for example, go skating, to the movies, or just hang out. Gradually, the numbers involved become smaller: perhaps three or four couples together, for comfort and protection; then, by high school, double or single dating. As in simple societies, gifts are exchanged: bracelets, pins, rings. The difference is that the gifts are exchanged by the dating couple and not by their families.

Then follows a period of semiengagement prior to the formal wedding announcement. Up to this time, either young person can be released from the relationship, not without pain, but with relative ease. Once the public announcement is made, families and friends and the world at large are witnesses to the intention to marry; larger and more expensive gifts are exchanged. These customs reinforce the process—followed in most societies—of progressively bringing the weight of the community to bear on mate selection. Marriage is still too important to families and societies to be left entirely to the engaged couple.

In contrast to marriage arranged by kinfolk, this pattern of mate selection can be described as relatively "free," but there are many ways in which such choices are channeled by parents and peers. Thus, although theoretically you could choose any one of hundreds of millions of persons of the opposite sex, you are confined to a rather limited subset: the people you actually meet and those whom you can confidently bring home to dinner. These factors alone automatically exclude all but a small "pool of eligibles"—people likely to be very similar to you in terms of social background characteristics.

The tendency to select a mate of the same race, religion, social class, ethnic group, educational level, and age as oneself is called **homogamy** (*homo* = "like"; *gamy* = "marriage"). People similar to oneself are easy to be with for a number of reasons. First of all, there is a foundation of shared values and attitudes as a result of similar socialization, which reduces the likelihood of disagreement and misunderstanding. Second, people who agree with us are very rewarding to be with because they reinforce our own sense of rightness. Third, we avoid negative reactions from family and friends.

Homogamy is the practice of selecting a mate with similar social background characteristics.

But modern societies provide widened opportunities for meeting people from different geographic areas and social backgrounds—at college, in the armed forces, at the workplace, in singles bars, and even through personal advertisements or video dating services. Women, in particular, have greater freedom than in the past to meet and date a variety of men. Thus, increasing numbers of American marriages are **heterogamous** (*hetero* = "different") in terms of race, religion, and ethnicity (Rytina et al., 1988). Heterogamy has its benefits in exposing marriage partners to other ways of thinking and doing, thereby adding an element of variety and challenge to the relationship.

Heterogamy is the practice of selecting a mate with different social background characteristics.

It has been generally assumed that homogamous marriages are somewhat more stable than heterogamous unions, and that cross-racial marriages are especially vulnerable, as are those that encompass wide differences in age, education, and social class. The data, however, are not altogether clear. In general, as barriers to heterogamy fall, couples are able to adjust and adapt more easily than when such unions were rare and subject to strong parental and peer disapproval.

The Family Cycle

Modernization has also brought changes in the timing of family events across the life course. Comparing the typical pattern of American families formed in 1900 with that of a couple marrying today, we can see how extensive these changes are. The 1900 marriage would have followed a rather long courtship period while the husband-to-be established himself economically; despite the long wait, both would enter marriage with limited sexual experience. The couple would probably have four children, the last being born when the mother was in her mid-thirties. By the time the youngest child was ready to leave home, it was likely that one parent had died. The widowed spouse would survive for a half-decade or more, often living with an unmarried child.

In contrast, couples today enter marriage after a short courtship and relatively long history of sexual experience. The childbearing phase of the family cycle will consist of two offspring, closely spaced, and be completed by the time the mother is age thirty. When the children are in school fulltime, if not before, the mother will reenter the labor force. The children will be out of the house—in college or living on their own—when the parents are in their early fifties (Teachman et al., 1987; Rindfuss et al., 1988). Given the great increase in life expectancy during this century, the parents will now enjoy at least *two decades* of being alone together again. This is a dramatic change, a phase of the life cycle— the **empty nest stage**—that did not exist for most couples in the past (Glick, 1989). The empty nest is typically followed by five to ten years of widowhood, as wives survive their husbands.

> The **empty nest stage** of the family cycle occurs when all the children are out of the house and the parents are alone together again.

The proportion of households occupied by a married couple has declined, while the proportions of single-person and single-parent households have risen.

Dual-Earner Families

Dual-earner families have become the new norm. Almost 60 percent of married women are now in the labor force, including more than 73 percent of those with school-age children and 57 percent of those with preschoolers (*Statistical Abstract, 1990,* p. 385). Families with two earners have significantly higher median incomes than do those with one earner. Employed wives tend to be in better emotional and physical health than nonemployed wives (although some of this difference may be due to the fact that healthier women will enter the labor force). At the same time, there are conflicting data on the effects of wives' employment on their husband's sense of well-being—some men will feel relief at sharing financial responsibility and enjoying a higher standard of living; others will find it difficult to give up traditional role expectations.

As for the effects of a wife's employment on the marriage relationship, dual-earner marriages do tend to be less stable than those with one earner (Raschke, 1987). But these data are difficult to interpret. Wives in less satisfying marriages may be most likely to seek employment; or, being employed and having financial security makes it possible for a woman to leave an unhappy marriage. A wife's labor-force participation does require adjustment as the power balance shifts, and there are problems of meshing work and leisure schedules with the demands of homemaking. One problem is finding time to spend together; the more time spent in joint activity, the more satisfying is the marital relationship of dual-earner couples (Kingston and Nock,1987). Finding time to spend with children is another concern, typically solved by a working mother's reducing time spent on marginal child care activities, such as clothes shopping and housekeeping, rather than increased time spent by fathers (Nock and Kingston, 1988).

The wife's gains in mental health and sense of control are partially offset by *role overload*, as most employed women also take full responsibility for household and child care tasks. The typical employed wife spends a total of 70 to 80 hours a week on work inside and outside the home. In this situation, a great deal of role negotiation must take place, as family members come to accept her employment and eventually to take it seriously (Hood, 1983). Couples that cannot negotiate a satisfactory adaptation will be under stress. If the wife leaves the labor force, she may become resentful; if she stays, other family members will feel neglected. Authentic role-sharing marriages are extremely difficult to achieve (Smith and Reid, 1986).

For many critics of the contemporary family, the major obstacle to the goal of gender equality is that women continue to perform the great majority of household and child care tasks, regardless of the time they spend in the paid labor force (Berk, 1985; Brannon and Wilson, 1987). Although there is some evidence that men are now spending more time doing housework and women less, these changes have taken place for *both* employed and nonemployed women (Kiker, 1988; Pleck, 1989). Gender differences in child care are equally persistent. Despite agreement with the ideal of shared child care, or at least of increased paternal involvement, relatively few men put it into action, even if they are willing (Hochschild and Machung, 1989).

However, there are signs of change. Traditional sex role attitudes are related to age and birth cohort, with new cohorts of young adults increasingly approving of shared roles, especially those in dual-earner families (Harris, 1987). As a consequence, many young couples will begin marriage with flexible role expectations. But attitudes also change in response to actual situations, so that couples who start out in traditional roles find themselves adopting different behaviors and beliefs during their marriage, depending on their work experience, whereas others who had expected greater sharing find themselves drifting into traditional patterns.

Although the change in women's roles has been gradual but constant over the past two decades, there is also evidence of important changes taking place for men, particularly younger men (Stein, 1984; Pleck, 1989). For example, one study shows that, compared to their fathers, young men held a more "nurturing" view of fatherhood, with less emphasis on the "provider" role (Pruett, 1987; Entwisle and Doering, 1988).

For children, their mother's employment has no strong or consistent negative effects (Piotrkowski et al., 1987; Gottfried and Gottfried, 1988). If the mother is working because she wishes to, if there is support from her husband and others, and if there are adequate child-care arrangements, the children's social and intellectual development is no different from that of children raised by full-time homemakers. However, questions about availability, adequacy, and affordability have elevated the issue of day care from a personal problem to a public issue (Galinsky and Stein, 1990).

Who's Minding the Children?

Almost 60 percent of all mothers of children under the age of six are in the labor force; half are full-time workers; and the great majority are either the sole support of their children or have a husband earning less than $20,000 per year. Who cares for their children?

The most recent data from the Bureau of the Census (1988) is shown in Figure 9-3. As you can see, fewer than one in four children is in an organized child care facility. Slightly

FIGURE 9-3 Primary child care arrangements used by working mothers for their children under five years old. Figures from winter 1984–85 have been rounded. (Source: U.S. bureau of the Census, P-70, No. 9, 1987.)

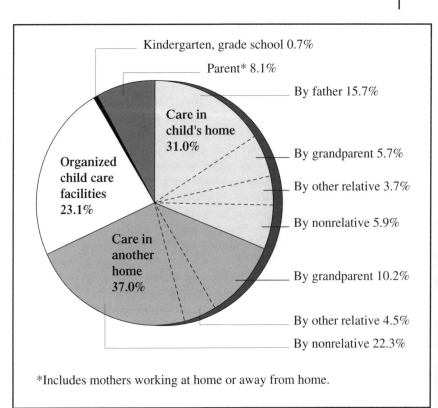

Kindergarten, grade school 0.7%
Parent* 8.1%
By father 15.7%

Care in child's home 31.0%

By grandparent 5.7%
By other relative 3.7%
By nonrelative 5.9%

Organized child care facilities 23.1%

Care in another home 37.0%

By grandparent 10.2%
By other relative 4.5%
By nonrelative 22.3%

*Includes mothers working at home or away from home.

less than one-third are cared for in their own home, often by a father while the mother works off-hour shifts. Close to 40 percent are cared for in the home of another person, often a relative, but most likely a paid but unlicensed day care worker.

The United States is one of the few modern industrial societies without a comprehensive system of child and family assistance; little federal aid is available.* However, some states have passed parental leave legislation. For example, Minnesota recently became the first state to require employers of 21 employees or more to offer up to six weeks of unpaid leave to both mother and father of a newborn. This type of legislation is fiercely opposed by Chambers of Commerce and other business groups, who claim that it would be a major expense for business in lost productivity, training new workers, and carrying health insurance costs. Nonetheless, a few major corporations have realized workers' needs for child care and have developed supportive policies (Auerbach, 1988).

Much resistance also comes from political and social conservatives who feel that child care is solely a parental responsibility and who fear the government's intrusion into the privacy of the family. Critics also worry about the long-term effects of any child care that is not provided by parents or grandparents.

On the other side, political liberals argue that worker morale would be strengthened and the rate of turnover reduced if child care were publicly funded and regulated; that day care centers are not necessarily inferior to a child's home, especially for the poor (Burchinal, 1987); and that families might actually be strengthened by government programs that encourage parental leave, as appears to be the case in Sweden (Moen, 1989).

Because the number of young mothers in the labor force is expected to continue to rise, and because many of you plan to combine work and child rearing, this is an issue you will be dealing with in the years and decades ahead. What child care policies would you prefer, and why?

---

*Family and Medical Leave Act: Effective August 3, 1993, employers with 50 or more employees are required to provide their employees with 12 weeks of unpaid leave during any 12-month period so that the employee can care for (1) his or her newborn child, (2) his or her newly adopted child, (3) his or her seriously ill spouse, son, daughter, or parent, or (4) his or her own serious health condition. Generally speaking, the employee is entitled to return to his or her job upon return to work, and the employer is required to maintain the employee's health care benefits during the time the employee is on leave.

Dual-Career Families

A variation on the dual-earner family is the **dual-career family** (Hertz, 1986; Scarf, 1987). Hertz interviewed well-to-do families whose joint incomes allowed them to buy the various support services that enabled both husband and wife to advance their careers and to have a comfortable life-style. Because careers are demanding, some stress still existed; couples had to work out a new set of expectations with regard to work and family obligations. Feminists, especially, find themselves in a dilemma because this new class of highly paid businesswomen depends on maintaining a large pool of lower-income women who work as domestics and child care givers.

Given the probably irreversible trend toward wives' employment, it is safe to predict increasingly egalitarian marriages, with a division of labor, both within and outside the home, more flexible than in our recent past. Among the new family life-styles that could become more common in the future are (1) the family organized around the wife's career—the "WASP" or "*Wife as Senior Partner*" pattern (Atkinson and Boles, 1984—in which a husband's job permits greater flexibility, the wife has a high-status position, and there are no young children in the household; and (2) the "**commuter marriage**," in which both partners are equally committed to their careers as well as to their marriage, but work in different cities (Gerstel and Gross, 1984). The commuter marriage usually involves two separate households with the partners alternating weekend visits. Both these variations on the dual-career model are extreme departures from normative expectations of the wife's role and have a number of built-in stresses. However, researchers have found that they also have compensations, including great flexibility in negotiating marital roles.

Dual-career families or couples are ones in which both husband and wife have a career.

Commuter marriages occur when husband and wife work in different cities and typically maintain separate households.

Men in Families

Traditionally, even in the sociology of the family, mention of husbands and fathers is usually confined to their role as major breadwinner. Only recently has a research literature emerged on such aspects of men's family roles as causes, correlates, and consequences of increased participation in parenting and homemaking (Lamb, 1986; Lewis and Salt, 1986; Chafetz, 1987; Franklin, 1988; Kimmel and Messner, 1989; Pleck, 1985, 1989).

The great majority of men will get married at least once, most will also become fathers, and a higher proportion of men than women, at all ages, will be married and living with a spouse. Clearly, family life continues to provide many comforts and benefits to men and may bring even more satisfaction to the men who participate most fully (Lewis, 1986).

The New Father. As part of the "natural childbirth" movement, increasing numbers of young husbands have joined their wives in birthing courses and taken part in the actual delivery. Although it is doubtful whether this experience alone creates a father-child bond of special strength, the men who choose this experience are likely to be different from those who do not in terms of attitudes and values related to child care.

A small proportion of new fathers will also assume a major role in caring for the infant (Risman, 1987; Kimmel and Messner, 1989). These men tend to be highly educated, married to women in high-status jobs, and to have flexible time schedules and an ideological commitment to gender equality (Russell, 1983). As much as many men might wish to take a more active role in child care, they are inhibited by the demands of outside employment. Employers could, if they valued the loyalty of employees (both men and women), lessen the conflict between work and family responsibilities by providing flexible work schedules, parental leave without loss of benefits, and educational programs at the workplace (Thorne, 1987).

The New Husband. As few employers offer such supports, and as time spent on family tasks brings lower rewards to men than to women, there has *not* been a major shift in the division of household labor over the past two decades, except, perhaps, in the "fun" parts of child care (Pleck, 1985; 1989).

The day of the "househusband" remains very distant. But if there are few men who are full-time child care givers or homemakers, there is no question that the division of household labor is becoming increasingly varied. The process of role negotiation will lead to many different outcomes, which can be seen as a strength rather than a weakness of our family system. In all its variety, the American family system has adapted to the conditions of postindustrial society. According to recent survey data, for most Americans intimacy and sharing are the goals of relationships, and family life continues to be the leading source of satisfaction; the vast majority of young people expect to marry and raise children.

Comprehension

True/False and Multiple Choice

Treat the following questions as test questions. Do not look back at the reading.

_____ 1. Although marriages in America are not *arranged* by parents, the parents can more or less direct their child's choice of a mate. (T/F)

2. Sara and Jim are engaged to be married. They both belong to the Catholic church, have college degrees, and come from upper middle class families. This match reflects the concept of
   a. homogamy
   b. polygamy
   c. heterogamy
   d. polyandry

3. Which of the following stages in the family life cycle did *not* exist for most married couples in 1900?
   a. the honeymoon
   b. the empty nest
   c. parenthood
   d. grandparenting

4. Approximately _____ percent of married women are now in the labor force.
   a. 73
   b. 60
   c. 55
   d. 45

_____ 5. Dual-earner marriages are more stable than marriages with just one wage earner. (T/F)

_____ 6. Husbands today, whether they are married to women who work outside the home or to women who are not employed, are doing more housework. (T/F)

_____ 7. The majority of working mothers with children under five use organized child care facilities. (T/F)

_____ 8. The "new father" is one who participates in the birthing process and so bonds immediately with the child. (T/F)

_____ 9. Men who participate in taking care of their babies tend to be more educated than men who do not. (T/F)

_____10. "Househusbands" are no longer rare in the modern family. (T/F)

Essay Questions

1. Why is it assumed that homogamous marriages are somewhat more stable than heterogamous marriages?
2. Define "gender equality." Define "role overload." Have American women achieved gender equality within the family? Support your answer with evidence from the reading.
3. "One study shows that compared to their fathers, young men held a more 'nurturing' view of fatherhood with less emphasis on the 'provider' role." Define *nurturing* and *provider* in this context.
4. Explain "WASP" in your own words. Make up an example.
5. Would "commuter marriages" be more at risk than other dual-income marriages? Why or why not?

Your Opinion: Discuss or Write

Do you think the changing roles of men and women in industrialized societies will have a positive or negative effect on the family? Explain your answer, using evidence from the two readings on the family (chapters 7 and 9).

10. Family Secrets

(by Ellen Goodman)

Preparing to Read

Americans place great value on *independence*. They are taught from childhood to "stand on their own two feet," not to depend on others. Older Americans have no less desire to be independent. They remain in their own homes as long as they are physically able. They do not want to live with their adult children; or as they put it, they do not want to be a burden to anyone.

Do the elderly in your culture feel the same way? Or do they expect and want to lean on their adult children? Do grandparents live with their children and grand-children?

The following essay by Ellen Goodman discusses older Americans' desire for independence. Ellen Goodman, a well-known syndicated newspaper columnist, writes about contemporary topics. In 1980, Ms. Goodman won a Pulitzer Prize in journalism. Pulitzer Prizes are awards given in the United States each year for distinguished achievements in journalism, literature, music, and the arts.

NOW READ THE ARTICLE THROUGH.

Family Secrets

by Ellen Goodman

1 BOSTON— My friends are at the age when we begin to talk less about child care and more about parental care. The subject of our lunchtime conversations has shifted. Once they leaned heavily toward pediatrics, now they include geriatrics. Our long-distance telephone checkups on each other's lives also run down a longer list. Once they accounted for sons and daughters. Now they include mothers and fathers.

2 In middle age, most of us are flanked by adolescent children and aging parents. We are the fulcrum of this family seesaw, expected to keep the balance. As one set of burdens is lifted gradually by independence, another is descending, sometimes slowly, sometimes abruptly, pulled by the gravity of old age or illness.

3 In the past year, a neighbor of mine has helped her son choose a college and her mother choose a retirement home. A friend who has just stopped accompanying her children to their doctor's appointments has begun driving her father to his. A colleague who filled her thirties with guilt about being a working mother is entering her fifties with guilt about being a working daughter. It's her parents who need her now.

4 It was to be expected, I suppose. After all, it is nothing more than the reality of the life cycle. But in fact it wasn't expected. Not really.

5 Like most Americans, my friends were raised to believe that independence was the norm. We learned to value it, nurture it, respect it, and demand it of ourselves and others. Today we "stand on our own two feet." It was hard for some of us to have that independence challenged by the helplessness of our children. It is much harder to see our parents become needful.

6 Some of this difficulty is familiar. . . . The child in us always wants our parents to be stronger, to be caretakers rather than caretaken. When we mother and father our mothers and fathers, we feel a bit like orphans.

7 But this stage of life, of mid-life, is also hard because many of our parents lied to us, just as we in turn lie to our children. Perhaps lie is too harsh a word, but let me explain.

8 In America today, it is considered neurotic, or at least unhealthy, to teach children that they owe us for their orthodontia,* their college tuition, their very life. We do not have children "to take care of us in our old age" anymore; at least we don't say that. The model of a sacrificial parent waiting for a return on her investment has become a satire. Raising them is supposed to be an act of free love.

9 So we tell the young that we need nothing in return. We free up their emotional inheritance so they can spend it on the next generation. At the same time we prepare for our own old age — buffer our lives against "needing" — with IRA's** and Social Security, with medical insurance and Medicare.***

10 But Social Security doesn't make telephone calls, and Medicare doesn't visit the hospital, and while independence extends longer and wider into the late decades now, only rare people leave this life without becoming somewhat dependent on others, especially their children.

11 The lie — that parents will remain independent — is not a malicious one. It's not even deliberate. It is believed when told by thirty-year-old fathers to eight-year-old sons, by forty-year-old mothers to twelve-year-old daughters. It is handed down in good faith by generations of parents when we are in our prime.

12 We believe our own lie because we cannot imagine — even those taking care of our own mothers and fathers — that it will happen to us. It is virtually impossible for a forty-five-year-old to know what he will be like at seventy-five, what he will want, what he will need, what he will resent. Yet by forty-five, he has seeded the ground for his own child's middle-aged shock.

13 Our terror of losing this prized American possession — independence — is what makes us define a good death as a sudden death. We choose to believe that we can avoid becoming a burden on our children. Our shame about aging prevents us from knowing and telling our children the dirty little secret of our human existence: When we too are old we may need them, need to lean on them.

14 Here, in the middle of life, we are just learning the truth from one generation, still hiding it from the next.

---

*orthodontia: branch of dentistry that deals with straightening teeth
**IRA: Individual Retirement Account: a means of saving money for the years after retirement
***Medicare: a U.S. government program that provides medical care for the aged

Comprehension

Questions and Discussion (Written or Oral)

Answer the following questions based on the information in the essay.

1. "The subject of our . . . conversations has shifted. Once they leaned heavily toward pediatrics, now they include geriatrics." (par. 1)
   a. To whom does "our" refer?
   b. *Pediatrics* is the science dealing with the medical care and diseases of children. *Geriatrics* is _____

   _____

2. "We are the fulcrum of this family seesaw. . . ." (par. 2)
   Explain paragraph 2 in your own words. Label the picture of the seesaw to illustrate your explanation.

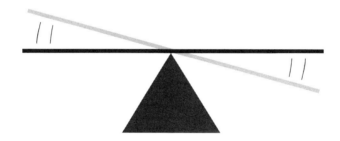

3. Americans are raised to stand "on their own two feet." What does this mean? Do you think this parental advice can have a *negative* as well as a positive effect on a person's life? Support your answer with evidence from the reading.

4. "When we mother and father our mothers and fathers, we feel a bit like orphans." (par. 6) This statement means
   a. When our parents die, we become orphans.
   b. When our parents become dependent on us, we feel like orphans.
   c. We feel sad when we can no longer take care of our parents.

   Explain your answer.

5. "Raising them is supposed to be an act of free love." (par. 8)
   This statement means
   a. "We do not have children 'to take care of us in our old age'...."
   b. Children should be raised to give freely of their love.
   c. Children should be taught to appreciate the sacrifices their parents made for them.

   Explain your answer.

6. Does Ms. Goodman think that Social Security and Medicare can take the place of children caring for aging parents? Why or why not?

7. Explain the meaning of the title "Family Secrets."

8. What is the main idea of this essay? A writer may repeat the main idea once or several times throughout a piece of writing. Read through the essay again and underline any phrase or sentence that expresses the main idea.

9. Ms. Goodman does not consider the *lie* that Americans tell their children evil or hateful. Why?

Reading Critically

— What do you think may have prompted Ellen Goodman to write this essay? (Read the first three paragraphs again.)

— Did she have a particular audience (readers) in mind when she wrote the essay?

— Read paragraph 13 again. Is there language in this paragraph that **implies** that America is a youth-oriented society? Explain your answer.

— Do you detect a note of sadness or anger or both in Ms. Goodman's writing? Explain your answer.

— What is the attitude of your society toward *aging* and the *aged?*

Vocabulary Study

Guessing the Meanings of Words from Context

Following are some excerpts from the reading selection. Try to guess the meaning of each circled word by studying the underlined words and phrases. You may want to work with a partner.

1. "In middle age, most of us are (flanked) by <u>adolescent children</u> and <u>aging parents</u>. We are the (fulcrum) of this family <u>seesaw</u>, expected to keep the <u>balance</u>." (par. 2)

    flank (v.): _____

    <u>ful</u>crum* (n.): _____

2. "Like most <u>Americans</u>, my friends were raised to believe that <u>independence</u> was the (norm.)" (par. 5)

    norm (n.): _____

3. "The <u>child</u> in us always wants our <u>parents</u> to be <u>stronger</u>, to be (caretakers) rather than (caretaken.)" (par. 6)

    <u>care</u>taker (n.): _____

    <u>care</u>taken (n.): _____

4. "When we too are old we may <u>need them</u>, need to (lean on) them." (par. 13)

    lean on (idiom): _____

Glossary

The numbers in front of the words indicate the paragraphs (in the reading) in which the words are found. Stressed syllables are underlined.

(8)	neu<u>rot</u>ic (adj.)	having a mild mental disorder
(8)	<u>sat</u>ire (n.)	(a work of) literature or art intended to show the foolishness of something in an amusing way
(11)	ma<u>li</u>cious (adj.)	bad, evil
(13)	<u>bur</u>den (n.)	great responsibility

---

*Stressed syllables of the circled words are underlined.

Pronoun Referents

The underlined pronouns here refer to nouns in the indicated paragraphs from "Family Secrets." Decide which nouns these are. Circle the letter next to the best answer or write your answer in the answer blank.

1. In paragraph 3, sentence 2, <u>his</u> refers to
   a. doctors
   b. appointments
   c. friend

2. In paragraph 5, sentence 2, <u>it</u> refers to _____.

3. In paragraph 8, last sentence, <u>them</u> refers to _____.

4. In paragraph 11, sentence 1, <u>one</u> refers to _____.

5. In paragraph 14, <u>it</u> refers to
   a. generation
   b. truth
   c. lie

11. A Sharp, Beribboned Message to Abusive Husbands

(by Joe Murray, Atlanta Journal*)*

Preparing to Read

Abuse—Injure, Harm, Hurt

If you read the newspapers or look at television, you know that a serious social problem in the United States is spousal abuse. What is *spousal abuse?* Is this a problem in your own country? What do you think can be done to prevent domestic violence?

Sometimes writers will deal with serious subjects in a humorous manner — a good way to capture the reader's attention. Humorist Joe Murray writes about an *abused* wife in the following story. Mr. Murray is a syndicated newspaper columnist who writes out of Texas.

Writing Your Own Ending to the Story

The last paragraph—the ending—of the story you are about to read has been deleted. After you read the story, write your own ending and then read it to your classmates. Your teacher will then tell you where to find the last paragraph of "A Sharp, Beribboned Message to Abusive Husbands."

NOW READ THE ARTICLE THROUGH.

Joe Murray
A sharp, beribboned message to abusive husbands

1 ANGELINA COUNTY, Texas—I read in the newspaper that the governor of Maryland freed eight women from prison—six of them convicted of murder—on the grounds that the victims were boyfriends or husbands who had been beating them up. I know a little something about that sort of thing.

2 It's a story that was told by a priest, so I guess it's true. This didn't happen way off in Maryland but right in the Pineywoods. It's not quite so current. The story goes back 40–50 years.

3 A nice young woman of the community had married a nice young fellow and moved off to the farm that he owned. Most everybody thought it was a fine match. But not so. It was an uneven match.

4 Not long after they were married she began to show bad bruises on her face and arms. When she walked, she was like a young person suddenly grown old. Some days she could barely hobble around.

5 Everybody who knew about it knew what was happening. Somebody should have done something about it, but no one did.

6 Finally, one evening when he had beaten her something fierce, and he had passed out drunk on the sofa, she waited until he was snoring his loudest and she was sure he was dead asleep.

7 She crept to the barn, she took down the long-handled axe that he kept there and then she marched back into the house, looking neither left nor right. This is what she did with the axe. She took good aim, drew the axe back slowly and brought it down with great strength of purpose. She split his head right half in two.

8 The sheriff investigated and learned what everybody already knew. Nobody was inclined to prosecute her. If anything they were a little ashamed of themselves. By doing nothing they had allowed it to happen. In a way they were no less guilty than she.

9 She went free, of course, and went about her life in the community as a respected widow woman. Everybody remembered what had happened, but nobody thought much about it. In a few years, she remarried. As before, her husband was known as a fine man, and folks considered it a nice match. An even match? No, I wouldn't say that.

10 For a couple of years, all seemed well and good in their marriage. Then one afternoon it happened all again as it had happened all before. She was bruised and battered, and her husband was drunk asleep. The difference was that they lived in town. They had no barn.

11 This time she had to walk to a hardware store. This time she had to buy an axe. She marched back home with a strength of purpose, looking neither left nor right.

12

Comprehension

Questions and Discussion (Written or Oral)

1. What do you think prompted Joe Murray to write this column? Do you think the story the author relates is true? Why or why not?

2. What is the meaning of "It was an uneven match"? (par. 3)

3. Why wasn't the woman prosecuted for murdering her first husband? The author writes that the people who knew she murdered her husband "were no less guilty than she." Explain.

4. Explain the end of the story.*

5. What makes this column humorous? The subject matter? The end of the story? The manner in which the writer narrates the story? Explain your answer.

6. Do you think the title of Mr. Murray's column appropriate? Explain your answer.

7. Define *child abuse*.

---

*If you can draw, use a picture to help you in your explanation.

Vocabulary Study

Guessing the Meanings of Words from Context

Try to guess the meanings of the following vocabulary items from their context. The numbers in front of the words indicate the paragraphs (in the reading) in which the words are found. Stressed syllables are underlined. Underline the words, phrases, or sentences in the reading that helped you guess the meanings. Work with a partner.

(3) match (n.): _____

(4) hobble (v.): _____

(6) pass out (idiom): _____

(7) barn (n.): _____

Review: Vocabulary

Each item in column (2) is related in some way to a word or phrase in column (1). Find the best matches, and record the letters of the correct answers in the answer blanks. Then *explain* each answer on a separate sheet of paper.

Example: *Geriatrics* is the branch of medicine dealing with the diseases and care of old people. Find *geriatrics* in list (1) and *over 65* in list (2).

(1)	(2)
_____ 1. abusive	a. alcoholic
_____ 2. geriatrics	b. traditional American family
_____ 3. pass out	c. long and happy marriage
_____ 4. at risk	d. children of single parents
_____ 5. demise	e. over 65
_____ 6. dual income	f. divorce
_____ 7. hobble	g. battered spouse
_____ 8. alimony	h. family-friendly company
_____ 9. fidelity	i. commuter marriage
_____ 10. flextime	j. poor economy
_____ 11. lay off	k. skiing accident

Review: Vocabulary

Fill in each blank in the following passage with the appropriate word or phrase from the list. *All* the words and phrases will *not* be used.

demise	grim	lean on
disrupt	guilty	orphan
dual-income	immune	radical
geriatric	laid off	stand on one's own two feet

Betty, who is married and has two children, is thinking seriously about getting a job outside the home. Her family would then become one of many _____ families in the United States. However, she has read the _____ statistics on the _____ of the traditional American family, and she hesitates to make such a _____ change in her life. Moreover, she would have to go back to college. She has been out of school for a number of years, but she feels that she would adjust quickly. She is an independent person whose parents taught her to _____ .

Betty wants to become a _____ nurse. She recently became an _____ when her parents were killed in a car accident, so she wants to help take care of old people.

Frank, Betty's husband, is very supportive of her plans. He feels that no one is _____ from being fired or _____ , and he would feel more secure if his wife were working. He assures Betty that there is no reason for her to feel _____ about becoming a working mother.

12. Chen Ning Yang

(Bill Moyers, A World of Ideas*)*

Preparing to Read

The following excerpt is from *A World of Ideas,* a collection of conversations broadcast on TV between Bill Moyers, a respected American journalist, and a number of outstanding thinkers.

Skimming

Skim the following excerpt from *A World of Ideas.* Then answer the following questions without looking back at the reading.

1. With whom is Mr. Moyers speaking? What is the subject of the conversation?

   _____

2. Which of the following countries are not mentioned specifically in this conversation?
   a. Japan
   b. Russia
   c. European countries
   d. United States
   e. China
   f. England

3. What do you think you are going to learn from this conversation?

   _____

   _____

   _____

Chen Ning Yang

P H Y S I C I S T

To Dr. Yang, science is as beautiful as poetry and as complex as religion. An American citizen, born and raised in China, "Frank" (after Benjamin Franklin) Yang is the Einstein Professor of Physics and heads the Institute for Theoretical Physics at the State University of New York at Stony Brook. In 1957 he and a colleague, T.D. Lee, won the Nobel Prize for Physics for overturning a long-held theory about symmetry in elementary particles.

1   MOYERS: A National Report Card was released not long ago by the Educational Testing Service. It said, "American students are remarkably limited in their knowledge of science and their ability to use what they know." And there was also an association that ranked teenagers in seventeen different countries, showing that the United States ranked last in biology, eleventh in chemistry and ninth in physics. What do these reports say to you?

1a   YANG: It's a reflection of the true state of affairs of the American educational system. By that I mean not only the schools, but also the social attitude toward education. This is a big and very complicated issue. But what is very easy to observe is that the kids from the Orient—from Japan, China, Taiwan, Hong Kong, and Korea—are more disciplined. They have a tendency to listen to the advice of their parents and their teachers and learn that one has to work hard before one can get some enjoyment. Here in America, the system is quite different. I noticed when my children were very little, I would say, "Perhaps you should do this." They said, "No, I don't want to do it." "Why not?" "Because it's boring." This concept that something may be boring, so I don't want to do it, does not exist with children in the Orient. There somehow society is structured differently. They hear different things. They, therefore, do not have the idea that they have to find instant gratification before they launch into something. Here the kids all want to see something immediately, to see the point. Often, that's not possible.

2   MOYERS: If your three kids had been raised in China instead of here on Long Island, how would their education have been different?

2a   YANG: I have speculated on this. I think they would be very different individuals today. They would have learned more things which require steady studying. They would be willing to be drilled. Of course, my wife and I try to say to them, "Look, this doesn't work. You've got to study hard." I think they listen to us, but having grown up in this environment, they have a different set of values. In this respect, the educational system in the Orient has a great advantage. One of the manifestations of that is what you referred to in this report—that if you take high school kids and give them science or mathematics quizzes, American kids on the average don't do as well.

3   MOYERS: Eleven students from a high school in New York City were named semifinalists in a science awards competition—all eleven of them were Oriental.

3a   YANG: The most important reason for this phenomenon is what we just referred to. Kids from babyhood in the Orient learn to be quiet, sit down, and work before they can get ahead. They take that naturally.

4   MOYERS: It's just what society expects of them, and they know this?

4a   YANG: Yes. Their parents, their neighbors, their friends—all say the same thing. But don't get me wrong. I'm not saying that that system is absolutely good for everybody. The other side of the coin is that kids trained in the Orient tend to be too timid, tend to say, "My God, there have been all these sages, all these saints, who have done this and that. Who am I?" So there's an attitude that they cannot do anything which would be truly important. This attitude prevents a number of them later from jumping over hurdles to make important contributions. We see this very clearly among our graduate students. The graduate students from the Orient are quieter and more willing to work, and they make very good grades, but they are somewhat restrained from making imaginative leaps.

5   MOYERS: You mean that if you give them a problem, they can solve it, but if you ask them to find the problem themselves, they have a harder time at it?

5a   YANG: Yes, because there is a tendency for them to automatically, subconsciously say, "I have to follow the rules. The rules have already been given." They don't want to contradict previous authors. They don't want to make jumps.

6   MOYERS: They're taught very early about the great teachers of Chinese history, philosophy, culture, and religion.

6a   YANG: Yes, everything, and not only Chinese. They are taught that there was Newton, there was Maxwell, there was Einstein—who are you to challenge any of these great people of the past? This produces a quieting influence, but it also produces too timid an attitude. This too timid attitude is a handicap later on in life when they want to be more creative or more imaginative.

7   MOYERS: So there's a trade-off. They get a more disciplined, determined student, someone who's willing to work hard for the payoff a long time from now. But they don't get the creative daring of the individual spirit that soars beyond the accepted boundary.

7a   YANG: Yes, and in this respect, the Orient is not the only example. If you'll compare the Orient with European cultures and American cultures, Europe is somewhere in between the two, maybe two-thirds of the way closer to the American culture than the Orient in this particular respect. The European students are usually better trained and less daring than American students.

8   MOYERS: What do you think explains the fundamental difference?

8a   YANG: I'm not a sociologist or a historian, but I like to speculate. I think America is a new country. It is a young culture. The spirit of the opening of the West is still with the Americans. This was even more clear to me when I first came to this country more than forty years ago. I was amazed, for example, when I came here, that some of my fellow American graduate students said that their parents did not approve of their going to graduate school. Why? Because a young man should go out and earn money. It's a very practical and

individual-based philosophy that had worked in America for a long time. In the last forty years America has grown older, so the respect for learnedness has increased. My belief is that as cultures age, they gravitate toward a greater respect for learning. You tell kids that you have to sit down and learn all these great things that people have said in the past.

9   MOYERS: What are the problems you see now in American culture?

9a   YANG: One problem, which we referred to earlier, is that kids are not patient enough to learn. Another phenomenon is that we have drug problems. And then there's theft. For example, libraries keep on losing books. All these phenomena are deeply related to the American concept that the individual is, in the final analysis, supreme. I'm not saying it is a wrong concept. I'm only trying to analyze. In China, you would say that in the final analysis, it is the society that's important, not the individual. This fundamental value judgment trickles down to everything.

10   MOYERS: Here in this society you are told that what you do is important, that you've got to get out on your own and make it and succeed, and nobody's there to help you. It's just the opposite in China. Your children would not have been told in China, "Well, you've got to make it on your own. Get out and break away and start out on your own."

10a   YANG: No, that is not the system. In fact, you don't even have to be told that. You feel it in your bones. You grow up with that environment.

11   MOYERS: What do you think we have to learn from the oriental approach to education? And what do they have to learn from us?

11a   YANG: Both questions are important. About the former problem, I don't know what to say. I've thought about it. I think it's a big problem. It's a social problem, not just an educational problem, and I have no wisdom to offer. About the latter question—what could the Chinese system learn from the American?—I have discussed this matter repeatedly with my graduate students here from China, with Chinese leadership, and with Chinese university administrators and professors and students. This is an easier problem. I try to encourage the Chinese students first to broaden their knowledge, not just try to learn what has been written down into books. If you look at the journals, you find newer knowledge which has not yet congealed. The Chinese system has a tendency to channel the students too much. You learn one book, and then another book, and then another book. You have blinders over your eyes. You don't try to look into other things. You're not told to think for yourself. There is the tendency to say that if you do this and that, you'll get the hang of it and the enjoyment of it. That works in a lot of the cases. As a consequence, the students tend to learn this and expect that they will be told what to think next.

12 MOYERS: What does this do to them psychologically, to always respect authority, to take the teacher's word for it, to follow the given path?

12a YANG: It has good and bad elements to it. The good element is that compared to their contemporaries in America, they know more because they have studied more, they have been drilled more. But the disadvantage is that when it comes to innovation, they are more handicapped. More than one graduate student from China and Taiwan in Stony Brook has come to me and said, "Professor Yang, I find it very strange that I was the best among my class in examinations, but now here I'm doing research work, and I find that these American students are much more lively, much better than I am." I think that is a true statement for many of them. We see here the two sides of this educational system's results. What I tell them is that you should make an effort to break out of this hold on you, to read more about things which you have not been told to read, to listen to seminars even if you don't understand. There is a very ancient Chinese saying which goes something like this: "If you know what you know, and know what you don't know, that is true knowledge." That philosophy has had a profound effect on the Chinese system and on Chinese society. As a child, you would be scolded if you pretended you knew a little bit more than you actually did. The advantage of this is that you are more solid. You don't open your mouth when you don't really know what's going on. The disadvantage of it is that you become afraid. If there's something which you don't quite know, you have a tendency to externalize it from yourself because you are afraid that if you tangle with it, it gets you into a situation where you are in a semi-knowing state, and that is not comfortable. I told my graduate students from China and Taiwan, "You must overcome this. You go to a seminar, and most of the time you don't quite understand what's going on. You don't have to be afraid. I go there, I also don't understand quite what's going on, but that's not necessarily bad because you go there a second time, and you find that you learn more." I call this learning by osmosis. Learning by osmosis is a process which is frowned upon in China. The reason that the Chinese graduate students are less daring is because they don't want to get mixed up with something they only half know. But in frontiers work, in research, you're always half knowing and half not knowing.

13 MOYERS: You get right here to the edge, and then you leap.

13a YANG: Yes, you leap, and you may see only vaguely what is going on, but you should not be afraid of that. That was one of the things I learned after I came to this country, especially from Edward Teller, who was my thesis adviser. Here's a man who has an enormous number of ideas. He probably has ten ideas every day. Nine and a half of them are not right. But if you only have half an idea which is right, that, of course, is a lot every day. Furthermore, he's not afraid to talk about them. This is the opposite to the Chinese attitude that I've been talking about. Teller grabs any person and says, "Look, this is a bright idea, and we'll discuss it." This greatly impressed me. It was a completely new system.

14 MOYERS: Of course, the whole history of Western science has been to go into the unknown and to challenge all authority and all assumptions and to take everything apart.

14a YANG: Yes, that's correct. Compared to the West, this spirit is not very much in evidence in the Chinese system.

15 MOYERS: But given what you say, I would expect the United States to be in a stronger position scientifically. Yet we're told over and over again that we're becoming a nation of scientific ignoramuses, that only ten percent of American high school students ever take a course in physics, and only seven percent of American kids learn enough science to perform well in college-level classes. This daring, this experimentation, this spirit of innovation and adventure does not seem to be taking hold down in the masses of American kids, particularly in regard to science.

15a YANG: Yes, that's a big problem and it has been discussed from all sides. It's a very tough problem. But in some senses I'm more worried about a related phenomena. You see, the lack of scientific knowledge on the part of the high school students is a dangerous thing, but nevertheless, American science is still extremely good. The cumulative knowledge and drive, the cumulative tradition and buildup of big centers, have made America today still a leader in most areas of scientific research. It's certainly true in mathematics. In physics, Western Europe is vaulting ahead beautifully, but the United States has stayed at least on a par. The point is that the American system is capable of producing enough very good people to sustain this frontiers effort for some time to come. I am not worried that the overwhelming position of the United States in most areas of scientific research will be seriously eroded in the next twenty years. But the general level of education and the general level of scientific knowledge among the general population—that is where there's a great worry.

Look at Japan. Japan today is an important industrial nation. It's a nation with no resources. It's a nation which was very poor immediately after the war. But today they excel in so many things. This does not mean that their science is on top of the world. They are formidable, but the level of basic science research of Japan does not yet rival that of the United States. How then did they achieve the present industrial strength? They achieved it because they have more educated people. They have more people who have real knowledge, not just diplomas. They have more people who have learned science. And, furthermore, there is a different attitude toward life and toward work. I read somewhere that eight percent of the things that come off American assembly lines have to be rejected. The corresponding number is less than half a percent in Japan. If you have these two societies competing with each other, it's obvious which one will win in terms of the volume of sale. That's what we are witnessing today.

16 MOYERS: Do you think that's because the Japanese are more scientifically educated than we are?

16a YANG: They are more educated, and in particular they are more scientifically educated. This is very clear. You look at all these tests that you were referring to, and Japanese kids do extremely well because they really learn in schools.

Here the kids don't learn in schools. There are a few very bright ones who somehow learn even in this morass. They are really brilliant, and they are nurtured by the American system of freedom, pushing for the individual achievements. They later rise to the top and either achieve something as a big organizer, or achieve something as a scientist. That's what's still sustaining the United States, and will sustain her for some time to come. But a modern society has to be built also on a general population which is knowledgeable and which has the right attitude. That's where I think the American future has the greatest dangers.

This is what she did with her axe. She tied a big red bow around it and she placed it above the mantle of the fireplace. When her husband finally woke up, that was the first thing he saw, and they lived happily ever after.—

(c1991.)

112

Comprehension

Questions and Discussion (Written or Oral)

1. Contrast the social attitude toward education of American students with that of Oriental students.

2. ". . . kids trained in the Orient . . . tend to say, 'My God, there have been all these sages, all these saints, who have done this and that. Who am I?'" What does "Who am I" **imply**? (Look up *sage* and *saint* in your English/English dictionary.)

3. Dr. Yang sees three problems in American culture that are related to the American concept that the individual is supreme. What are the three problems, and do you agree with Dr. Yang that these problems are related to the individual-is-supreme concept?

4. "'If you know what you know, and know what you don't know, that is true knowledge.'" What adverse effect has this ancient Chinese philosophy had on Chinese society, students in particular?

5. Why does Dr. Yang consider American science "still extremely good" although "we're told over and over again that we're becoming a nation of scientific ignoramuses"? Then what is Dr. Yang worried about?

6. According to Dr. Yang, how did Japan become such an important industrial nation?

7. Go to the library and look up *Nobel Prize* in an encyclopedia.
   a. What are Nobel Prizes?
   b. In what fields are they given?
   c. Name *five* recipients of the Nobel Peace Prize in the last decade.

Vocabulary Study

Paraphrasing

Paraphrasing is restating a sentence or sentences in your own words in order to better understand difficult material.

The first step in paraphrasing is to know the meanings of the difficult words or phrases in a sentence. Guess the meanings of the circled words or phrases in the following excerpts by looking at the underlined portions of the excerpts. Then paraphrase the excerpts. Work with a partner.

1. "They [kids from the Orient] . . . learn that <u>one has to work hard before one can get some enjoyment</u>. . . .They, therefore, do not have the idea that they have to find instant gratification before they launch into something. <u>Here the kids all want to see something immediately</u>, to <u>see the point</u>. . . ." (par. 1a)

   _____

   _____

   _____

   _____

2. "They would have learned more things which require <u>steady studying</u>. They would be willing to be drilled. . . ." (par. 2a)

   _____

   _____

   _____

   _____

3. "The graduate students from the Orient are quieter and more willing to work,
   . . . but they are somewhat restrained from making imaginative leaps. . . .
   [They] say, 'I have to follow the rules. . . .' They don't want to contradict
   previous authors. They don't want to make jumps. . . . This too timid attitude
   is a handicap later on in life when they want to be more creative or more
   imaginative." (pars. 4a,5a,6a)

   _____

   _____

   _____

   _____

4. "Here in this society [U.S.] you are told that what you do is important, that
   you've got to get out on your own and make it and succeed, and nobody's there
   to help you. . . ." (par. 10)

   _____

   _____

   _____

   _____

5. "The Chinese system has a tendency to channel the students too much. You
   learn one book, and then another book, and then another book. You have blinders over your eyes. You don't try to look into other things. You're not told to
   think for yourself. . . . if you do this and that, you'll get the hang of it and the
   enjoyment of it. . . ." (par. 11a)

   _____

   _____

   _____

   _____

6. "The <u>cumulative</u> knowledge and drive, the <u>cumulative</u> tradition and buildup of big centers, have <u>made America today still a leader in most areas of scientific research</u>. . . . <u>In physics, Western Europe</u> is vaulting ahead beautifully, but the <u>United States has stayed</u> at least on a par. . . ." (par. 15a)

_____

_____

_____

_____

Glossary

The numbers in front of the words indicate the paragraphs (in the reading) in which the words are found. Stressed syllables are underlined.

(7)	<u>pay</u>off (n.)	outcome, consequence
(8a)	<u>grav</u>itate (v.)	to be drawn toward
(11a)	con<u>geal</u> (v.)	to become permanent
(12a)	inno<u>va</u>tion (n.)	introduction of something new
(12a)	os<u>mo</u>sis (n.)	a gradual absorption
(15a)	<u>cu</u>mulative (adj.)	increasing steadily in amount; accumulated
(15a)	e<u>rode</u> (v.)	become less gradually
(15a)	<u>for</u>midable (adj.)	powerful; of great strength
(16a)	mo<u>rass</u> (n.)	any confusing or troubling situation
(16a)	<u>nur</u>ture (v.)	support

13. Home Is the Key to Our Kids' Success in School

(by William Raspberry)

Preparing to Read

Nathan Caplan, Marcella Choy, and John Whitmore of the University of Michigan made a study of the academic achievement of the children of Indochinese "boat people" in American schools. You will read an excerpt from their research findings in chapter 16. In the late 1970s and early 1980s, many Vietnamese, Lao, and Chinese-Vietnamese families were forced to find refuge in the United States. The children of these refugees lost months and in some cases years of formal schooling while living in relocation camps. The research showed that "despite their hardships and with little knowledge of English, the children quickly adapted to their new schools and began to excel."

The following reading by William Raspberry is based on the research by Caplan, Choy, and Whitmore. Mr. Raspberry writes about contemporary issues and is a Pulitzer Prize winner in journalism.

READ THE ARTICLE THROUGH.

William Raspberry

Home Is the Key to Our Kids' Success in School

1 WASHINGTON—There's a simple truth about schools that you won't find in any of those studies on school reform. You won't find it in the reports detailing how poorly our children are doing in comparison with the children of Taiwan or Denmark. I know only two places where you can find it: in your own head, where the knowledge has lain for as long as you can remember, and in the February issue of Scientific American.

2 Here it is: America's schools are doing a pretty good job of teaching children who come to school ready for learning. Now if you and I know that, why is it that the people in charge of educational policy can't figure it out? The reason, I suspect, is that we tend to go searching for answers before we reach agreement on what the questions are.

For some, the question may be how to eliminate the problems of race in our society, or how to raise the test scores of black and Hispanic children. For others, it may be how to get children more interested in math and science. For still others, it may involve better preparation for entry-level jobs.

With so many questions, it is not surprising that the only thing we can agree on is that something is wrong. There's truth in that, but there is also truth in what you suspect and what teachers know: that much of what we talk about in our discussions of school failure has little to do with what happens at school and a lot to do with what happens at home.

Nathan Caplan, Marcella Choy and John Whitmore of the University of Michigan set out to explore reasons for the academic success of the children of Indochinese boat people in American schools. But their research leads them to a secondary conclusion: that "the American school system has retained its capacity to teach, as it has shown with these refugees. We believe that the view of our schools as failing to educate stems from the unrealistic demand that the educational system deal with social service needs."

6 The more you require schools to feed children, protect them from drugs and violence, look after their health and coach them in safe sex, the less time and energy the teachers will have left for academics.

7 The authors do not dismiss the importance of the social services schools are called upon to deliver; they simply insist that we separate teaching from social services.

8 One social service that needs to become a matter of routine is teaching parents how to get their children ready for school. I'm talking about parenting classes for those who already are parents and parenting courses for junior-high and high-school students. Most of them will be parents, so they may as well learn something about being good parents.

9 That one innovation might do more to improve school outcomes than all the reform recommendations that occupy so much of the debate. That's not to say that the schools don't need improvement—only that there are some things that have to be done at home.

10 But you knew that.—(c1992.)

Comprehension

Recognizing the Topic

What is the *topic* or *subject* of the column by William Raspberry?

a.   education in America
b.   why America's children are failing in school
c.   social services in the schools in America
d.   the need for parenting courses in America's schools

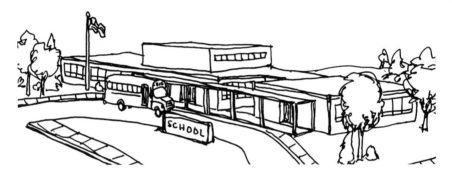

Recognizing the Main Idea

What is the *main idea* or the *main point* of Mr. Raspberry's column? (What is the writer saying about the topic? What point is he making about the topic?) In a sentence or two, write the main idea of the column.

_____

_____

_____

_____

Note: A writer will express the main idea *more than once* in a piece of writing. Scan the column and underline any phrase or sentence that expresses the main idea.

Comprehension

Questions and Discussion (Written or Oral)

1. Explain how the research conducted by Caplan, Choy, and Whitmore leads them to conclude that America's schools are still capable of teaching.

2. What do the researchers see as the answer to America's school problems?

Reading for Inferences

An *inference* is a *conclusion* made by a reader about what is *suggested* or *implied* in a reading passage. In other words, to **infer** is to "read between the lines."

Explain how the following statements can be **inferred** from Mr. Raspberry's commentary.

1. The general public knows what is wrong with America's schools. (What evidence is there in par. 1 and in the last sentence of the reading to lead to this conclusion?)

2. Mr. Raspberry based his column on an article in *Scientific American.* (Can you also **infer** that *Scientific American* is a magazine? Explain your answer.)

3. The children who need "social services" are children of low-income families.

4. Teachers in some American schools have to be substitute parents.

5. The role of the family is the key to the academic success of the children of the Indochinese "boat people."

6. "America's schools are doing a pretty good job of teaching children who come to school ready for learning" (par. 2). What does "ready for learning" **imply**?

14. Parents, Get Serious about Raising Your Kids

(by Joanne Jacobs, San Jose Mercury News*)*

Comparison and Contrast (Discuss or Write)

Read the following article by Joanne Jacobs. Do William Raspberry and Joanne Jacobs share any similar ideas? In what ways do they differ? Choose specific statements from each article of commentary to support your comparisons and contrasts.

Joanne Jacobs
Parents, get serious about raising your kids

1 SAN JOSE, Calif.—Parents, talk to your children. Talk to them about school. What are they learning? What's hard? What's fun? Talk to them about their friends. Tell them what you value. Tell them what you expect. Turn off the TV. Disconnect the Nintendo.

2 Do you want to know what teachers, principals and superintendents are saying about you, parents? They're saying: We know parents are busy. But we wish they'd spend more time with their kids. We wish they'd model responsible behavior. We wish they'd talk more. Kids are coming with values shaped by TV, video games and other children.

3 Schools are coping with the children of the post-Ozzie American family.* Two jobs: No time. One parent: No time, no money. No parent: No hope. Our schools were set up to teach reading, writing, 'rithmetic, civics and science, not to raise everybody's children. They are not very good at child-raising, but they believe they have to try.

4 If the kids are coming to school hungry, start a school breakfast program. If they're coming dirty, let them take showers at school. Buy socks and underwear. Take class time to talk about sexual behavior and substance abuse, if parents aren't handling it. Spend time on self-esteem-boosting exercises, if parents don't give their children a sense of self-worth. It won't work, but try.

5 Schools can't do everything. They can't afford to keep spending education money on proxy parenting and social services. It's costing a lot, and it's not working. What does work? Students who take more academic courses learn more than those who don't.

6 Parents, that means you've got to get serious about your child-raising values. Parents set the expectations, which are high. They set family rules. They value their family's culture and refuse to let their children drift or drown in the sea of popular culture.

7 Some parents are raising children who excel academically. Most of them are named Wang, Nguyen or Srinivasan.

8 Asian-American students were much more likely to say they wanted good grades to make their parents proud of them, or to show their love for their parents.

9 "When I was little my parents always said that they love me and that we should try our best to show we love them," wrote Kami Nguyen. Now, "they know when I get a bad grade I feel guilty so they don't worry."

10 Naved Zuroni believes it's his mission to fulfill his parents' dream, a good education for their children.

11 Bruce Zazueta (you don't have to be Asian) can envision the pride his parents will feel when he graduates from college.

12 I asked Nansi Nguyen if honor students get teased. "I don't care if they do," she said. "Let's see what happens when we grow up."

13 Nansi, Kami, Naved and Bruce will grow up just fine. How about your kids?—(c1993.)

Joanne Jacobs is a columnist for the San Jose (Calif.) Mercury News.

Ozzie and Harriet was a TV situation comedy depicting the ideal family of the 1950s.

15. Our Children & Our Country

(by William J. Bennett)

Summary Writing

A *summary* is a *condensation,* in *your own words,* of a reading selection. How do you *shorten* a reading? You omit the *unimportant details* and *concentrate on* the *main ideas* or *main points.* Here are some steps to follow when you write a summary.

1. *Skim* the selection before you read for thorough comprehension.

2. *Underline* the *main ideas* in the selection. (You may want to mark through the unimportant details.)

3. Write a good topic sentence.

4. Write your summary. Remember to *omit unimportant details, concentrate on main ideas,* and *use your own words.* (It might be necessary to repeat a few words and phrases from the selection.)

5. Do *not* express your opinion; a summary is *not* a response.

The following two excerpts are from the book *Our Children & Our Country,* by Dr. William J. Bennett, former U. S. Secretary of Education. In his book, Dr. Bennett analyzes American schools and culture and argues that American education *can* work better.

Summarize the following excerpt in not more than four sentences.

Our Children & Our Country
by William J. Bennett

The plight of the family has been much discussed in the media. It is by now well known to all. The research on this problem is clear: Take one of the parents permanently out of the home, and the educational health of the child is likely to suffer. Children from single-parent homes are more likely to have lower grades, more likely to be discipline problems in the classroom, more likely to skip school, to be expelled, and to end up as dropouts. They are more likely to experience emotional or psychological disturbance, to become involved with drugs, to get in trouble with the law.

This is not to say that a single parent cannot do a good job of raising children. Many do; they deserve our thanks and our praise. I have thanks and praise for one in particular: my mother, a divorced parent, who raised my brother and me. But it is obvious— it was obvious to me, and it was obvious to my mother— that it is much harder for one parent to raise a child than it is for two. This is another stubborn fact; it is simply a matter of having to spread oneself too thin.

The decline of the traditional American family constitutes perhaps the greatest long-term threat to our children's well-being. This country must not lose the most important educational institution of all, the one that has sustained and advanced our best ideals as a culture and as a civilization. This country must not lose the institution that has the unparalleled capacity to protect and nurture our children.

Summarize the following excerpt. Your summary should contain approximately one-fourth the number of words as the excerpt.

Our Children & Our Country
by William J. Bennett

The most sublime, the most solemn responsibility of our elementary schools is to teach children to read. When a school graduates a child who cannot read, that school has failed in its responsibility to the child and to the community. Studies show that today's elementary schoolchildren are better readers than those of fifteen years ago. According to the latest study by the National Assessment of Educational Progress, nearly 94 percent of nine-year-olds today possess rudimentary reading skills: they are able to follow written directions; they can match a picture with a written description. Yet, as they grow older, their performance falls well below what we should expect. According to the National Assessment of Educational Progress report, 40 percent of thirteen-year-olds lack the intermediate reading skills necessary to handle the books and lessons that we would expect a seventh- or eighth-grade teacher to assign. Most minority children fall below that intermediate level.

Teaching children to read is not a mysterious science. We know how it's done. We do it successfully all the time. We know, for instance, that children get a valuable start when their parents or other adults read to them at home. It helps when they are exposed to books from an early age. We know that a mixture of formal and informal instruction may be undertaken as early as kindergarten.

And we know that for most children, the most effective method for teaching reading is that which first teaches children the relationship between letters and sounds. This method is known as "phonics." From the 1920s to the early 1970s, a method known as "look-say" prevailed in our schools. It relied on children's memorizing the appearance of entire words. This method has proven considerably less effective than phonics.

Perhaps most important in teaching reading is the simple fact that children learn to read by reading. Books should occupy a central place in the home and the classroom; they should always be within children's reach. We should make sure that every schoolchild has a library card—and uses it.

Finally, let's make sure the books we provide our children are well written and interesting. Children may be discouraged from reading by the deadening prose and content of texts currently assigned in our elementary schools. Given our rich cultural heritage, this is inexcusable. Schools should compete for the attention of the mind and heart by offering the best that we have. Let's have our children read books like *Where the Wild Things Are, Winnie the Pooh,* and *Swiss Family Robinson.*

Summary of the Excerpt on Page 126: Two Samples

Summary 1

Research has shown that children from single-parent homes suffer many problems including educational difficulties related to school and emotional difficulties related to drugs or crime.

Not all single families will have problems; however, raising a child as a single parent poses more difficulties than sharing that responsibility with another person.

It is important that the traditional American family of two parents and children not die. It is the family that can best educate our children and help them through the difficulties of childhood.

Summary 2

Dr. Bennett states that although many single parents bring up their children successfully, research shows that children from single parent homes are more likely to have problems in school as well as psychological problems. He therefore warns that the traditional American family must be preserved in order to "protect and nurture our children."

16. Indochinese Refugee Families and Academic Achievement

(by Nathan Caplan, Marcella H. Choy, and John K. Whitmore)

Summary Writing

The following excerpt is from "Indochinese Refugee Families and Academic Achievement," an article that appeared in *Scientific American*. The authors, Nathan Caplan, Marcella H. Choy, and John K. Whitmore, made a study of Indochinese refugee resettlement while working together at the Institute for Social Research at the University of Michigan at Ann Arbor.

Write a summary of the *first five paragraphs* of the excerpt, following the steps to summary writing. (Even though you are going to summarize only five paragraphs, read the *entire* excerpt carefully.) Before you begin writing, you may want to discuss what you have read with a partner.

Indochinese Refugee Families and Academic Achievement
(by Nathan Caplan, Marcella H. Choy, and John K. Whitmore)

1 Nowhere is the family's commitment to accomplishment and education more evident than in time spent on homework. During high school, Indochinese students spend an average of three hours and 10 minutes per day; in junior high, an average of two and a half hours; and in grade school, an average of two hours and five minutes. Research in the U.S. shows that American students study about one and a half hours per day at the junior and senior high school levels.

2 Among the refugee families, then, homework clearly dominates household activities during weeknights. Although the parents' lack of education and facility with English often prevents them from engaging in the content of the exercise, they set standards and goals for the evening and facilitate their children's studies by assuming responsibility for chores and other practical considerations.

3 After dinner, the table is cleared, and homework begins. The older children, both male and female, help their younger siblings. Indeed, they seem to learn as much from teaching as from being taught. It is reasonable to suppose that a great amount of learning goes on at these times—in terms of skills, habits, attitudes and expectations as well as the content of a subject. The younger children, in particular, are taught not only subject matter but how to learn. Such sibling involvement demonstrates how a large family can encourage and enhance academic success. The familial setting appears to make the children feel at home in school and, consequently, perform well there.

4 Parental engagement included reading regularly to young children—an activity routinely correlated to academic performance. Almost one half (45 percent) of the parents reported reading aloud. In those families, the children's mean GPA was 3.14 as opposed to 2.97 in households where the parents did not read aloud. (This difference, and all others to follow in which GPAs are compared, is statistically reliable.) It is important to note that the effects of being read to held up statistically whether the children were read to in English or in their native language.

5 This finding suggests that parental English literacy skills may not play a vital role in determining school performance. Rather, other aspects of the experience—emotional ties between parent and child, cultural validation and wisdom shared in stories read in the child's native language, or value placed on reading and learning—extend to schoolwork. Reading at home obscures the boundary between home and school. In this context, learning is perceived as normal, valuable and fun.

6 Egalitarianism and role sharing were also found to be associated with high academic performance. In fact, relative equality between the sexes was one of the strongest predictors of GPA. In those homes where the respondents disagreed that a "wife should always do as her husband wishes," the children earned average GPAs of 3.16. But children from homes whose parents agreed with the statement had an average GPA of 2.64. In households where the husband helped with the dishes and laundry, the mean GPA was 3.21; when husbands did not participate in the chores, the mean GPA was 2.79.

7 This sense of equality was not confined to the parents—it extended to the children, especially in terms of sex-role expectations and school performance. GPAs were higher in households where parents expected both boys and girls to help with chores. Families rejecting the idea that a college education is more important for boys than for girls had children whose average GPA was 3.14; children from families exhibiting a pro-male bias had a mean GPA of 2.83.

Review: Vocabulary

Fill in each blank in the following passage with the appropriate word or phrase from the list. Use the correct tenses of the verbs. *All* the words and phrases will *not* be used.

channel	gravitate	osmosis
contradict	ignoramus	payoff
drill	nurture	soar
gratification	on his own	the hang of it

When David was in high school, he studied very little. He was impatient; he

had to find instant _____. However, he made good grades. He attended

classes regularly and seemed to learn by _____. When he was gradu-

ated, he was anxious to get out _____, but

his parents insisted that he go to college.

At the university, he gave more time to his stud-

ies. Although he often _____ his teach-

ers if he disagreed with their ideas, they liked and respected him. He _____

toward the law, and in his senior year, he applied to law school.

David knew he was no _____, but he was terribly afraid he would do

badly on the LSAT*. His spirits _____, however, when his friends and

teachers _____ his hopes and dreams. He _____ all his ener-

gies into studying for the LSAT.

The _____ for David's hard work was a high score and admittance

to the law school of his choice.

_____
*Law School Admission Test

The following two supplementary readings, *"Healthy Korean Economy Draws Immigrants Home"* and *"The Decay of Families Is Global, Study Says,"* continue with the themes of Immigration (Unit 2) and Family (Unit 3). Each selection is followed by a few questions to test reading comprehension and by a glossary.

Healthy Korean Economy Draws Immigrants Home

By PAM BELLUCK

1   Four years ago, Chang Hyeok Soo began making plans to leave Korea and move to the United States. He wanted to echo the success of his sister and brother-in-law, who had built a comfortable home in New Jersey and a thriving trading company in Manhattan.

2   But Korea's economic explosion made Mr. Chang, 29, change his mind. He took a trainee job with a Korean oil company and, in only a few years, his salary more than doubled.

3   Thirteen time zones away from Seoul, pinched between the handbag racks and costume jewelry cases in his Washington Heights shop, Suzy's Accessories II, Cha Soon Giel is closing up and returning to Korea after 23 years in New York. Rent increases and an ailing mother back home have persuaded him it is time to leave.

4   "I'm here, the mom-and-pop owner, and I am not sure I can make it much longer," said Mr. Cha, 53. "And since my mother country is now changing a lot, I will be happy to go back and see if there is a good opportunity there."

5   As Koreans poured into this country over the last two decades, their entrepreneurial energy transformed whole neighborhoods in New York and other cities. Now, with the burgeoning economy in Korea providing more opportunities there, Koreans have fewer reasons to move to the United States. And thousands of Koreans who raised families and built businesses here are returning to their homeland, some of them driven away by economic difficulties and others parlaying success in this country into better jobs in Korea.

6   Over the last five years, the number of people in South Korea who received immigration visas to the United States has fallen by more than half, from about 25,500 in 1990 to about 10,800 in 1994, according to the Bureau of Consular Affairs of the State Department. The flow of people returning to Korea jumped after the Seoul Olympics in 1988, according to the Korean Ministry of Foreign Affairs, which reported that in each of the last four years, between 5,000 and 6,500 people have gone back, compared with about 800 in 1980.

7   In 1987, the peak year for Korean immigration to the United States, one Korean moved back for roughly every 10 of the more than 30,000 who got visas to move to the United States. Last year, however, one person returned for about every two who came, the ministry reported.

8   Those who are returning say they are motivated by a cultural, social and economic stew of hopes and dissatisfactions. Some say they have never felt completely comfortable with the English language and the American culture, which many see as too unruly and informal. Others have become increasingly concerned about racial friction, violence and crime. And some want to contribute to the return of democracy in Seoul, where the military government was toppled in 1987.

9   But underscoring it all is the economic dynamism of Korea over the last five years and the recent recession in the United States. Seoul is becoming a major player in the global trading game. The value of its exports was the 12th largest in the world last year, according to International Monetary Fund reports.

10   The country's prosperity, however, has had one drawback for Koreans who want to return: Some say they can't afford to because apartments are getting so expensive.

A Glass Ceiling
For Professionals

11   Still, many Koreans, especially men who shunted their professional backgrounds to become merchants here, felt they could never achieve the social status they once had in Korea. Even some Koreans who have achieved considerable success here said they felt it would be difficult to rise higher in American companies, while their knowledge of English and the United States made them highly prized in Korea.

12   A gift shop owner from the Chicago suburbs has a contract to open an American coffee franchise in downtown Seoul. A professor at Cornell University Medical Center became chairman of the life sciences department at a Korean university, and staffed his entire department with Korean-American professors.

13   A second-generation Korean-American said he would probably move to Korea after graduation from law school because "a Harvard law degree goes much further in Korea than it does in America."

14   Even Mr. Chang's father-in-law, Suk K. Lee, who was chairman of the Korean-American Chamber of Commerce in New York, returned to Korea a few years ago to start a cable television company with other "Korean-New Yorkers."

15   And the governors of two of Korea's nine provinces were, until recently, American citizens: an economics professor from Rutgers University and a businessman who spent 20 years selling handbags and wigs in Manhattan. The businessman, Kim Hyuk Kyu, is already bringing a touch of New York to South Kyongsang Province. One of his first steps will be to paint all the taxicabs yellow.

16   "The reason people move is what's going on at home," said Philip Kasinitz, a sociology professor at Hunter College. "What's going on at home is the Korean economy is so strong that it's attracting the people who both have made it here and those who can't make it."

17   It is not clear how many Korean small businesses in New York are failing. Some merchants close one store and later open another. But these days, Korean dry cleaners, groceries and other small businesses are bumping up against a market they helped saturate, Dr. Kasinitz said.

18   "Pick stores in any neighborhood and ask them how business is," said Sung Soo Kim, the president of the Korean American Small Business Service Center of New York, in Flushing, Queens. "Half of them will say it's break-even or getting worse."

19   Stephen Lynton, a research associate with the Columbia University Center for Korean Research, said Korean businesses "fail all the time because Koreans tend to migrate toward high-risk businesses. Some people just give up and go home."

20   Some of those who give up feel great embarrassment. Mr. Cha said one friend who is moving back because his Washington Heights store is in trouble "is ashamed to admit that he was not accepted here."

21   But as many or more of those who are returning to Korea are not abandoning failure, but building on their successes in this country.

Comfort of Home
Is Part of the Draw

22   Until last year, Jhinu Christopher Jung was a lawyer in midtown Manhattan, working mostly for Korean-American clients. He was putting together a new law firm with about 10 other lawyers.

23   "All of a sudden I realized that I really didn't want to do that," Mr. Jung, 40, said in a telephone interview from Seoul, where he is setting up an international consulting firm. "In New York, I was becoming a sort of community lawyer—divorces, minor criminal matters, small business claims. But I wanted to do more international work and I felt I was sort of trapped. I felt that in the long run, if I were in Korea, I would be much better positioned than if I was in New York."

24   There was another reason, too.

    "I'm perfectly comfortable in New York," said Mr. Jung, who came to the United States when he was 14 and speaks excellent English. "But in some ways I felt culturally, linguistically and traditionally that I was much more Korean than I ever realized before."

25   Some of those who return to Korea say they always dreamed of retiring to their homeland after they raised children and educated them in American schools. And some are fulfilling Korean traditions of filial responsibility, taking care of elderly parents back home.

26   Others said that the Los Angeles riots and robberies of Korean stores in New York have made them more aware of racial conflicts and what they see as a lack of police responsiveness.

27   "After the L.A. riots, we have to live in a sort of racial tension, you know," said Mr. Cha. "In Korea, we are homogeneous, only one race. We never had experience living with others."

Korean Work Ethic
Left Mark on City

28   The wave of Korean immigration in the 1970's and 1980's transformed cities like New York as few other recent immigrant groups have. Koreans, many

of them highly educated professionals in their own country, seemed to patent a brand of hard work and enterprise that turned blocks in Harlem and Bedford-Stuyvesant, Brooklyn, and whole neighborhoods like Flushing, into bustling quarters of commerce.

29   Korean immigrants virtually invented the nail salon and reinvented the corner grocery—adding salad bars, deli counters, and bunches upon bunches of colored carnations and gladioluses.

30   "The Korean population has had a very substantial impact, a disproportionate impact because of its rate of self-employment," said Mitchell L. Moss, director of the Taub Urban Research Institute of New York University. "They succeeded beyond all standards and expectations, very rapidly."

31   Other immigrant groups have left the United States when changes in their native countries made it possible or advantageous to return, Dr. Moss and other sociologists said. They predicted that the Korean impact on New York will not really diminish, but over the years is likely to change.

32   Members of other immigrant groups will probably take over some Korean stores. The children of Korean immigrants, many of them well educated, are likely to move into professional jobs, law firms, technology, international trade. And Koreans will increasingly leave the cities.

33   "They're already moving out to the suburbs when they can," said Dr. Lynton. "It used to be that Koreans were very focused in urban population areas. Now, they're everywhere, even the smallest towns."

34   Moon In Soon, who is leaving Northbrook, Ill., to set up a Gloria Jean's Gourmet Coffee franchise in Seoul, said that like many other reverse immigrants she is keeping her American citizenship.

35   Some repatriates have had trouble adjusting. But things are getting easier. "The international community in Korea is getting rather large," said Dr. Lynton, "so that people who move back do not feel as alienated as they did before."

36   Others are facing unexpected challenges.

    Mr. Kim, for example, the governor of South Kyongsang Province, said taxi drivers are vigorously opposed to his efforts to transplant a bit of the flavor of midtown Manhattan.

37   "They do not like the brightness of the color yellow," Mr. Kim said. "They are saying it is not very healthy, that it hurts the vision."

Comprehension

Recognizing the Topic

What is the *topic* or *subject* of the article you have just read? Ask yourself, "What is the article about?" Choose the best answer.

a. Korean immigrants in the United States
b. declining Korean immigration to the United States
c. why Korean immigrants are leaving the United States to return to Korea
d. effects of Korean immigration on U.S. cities

Recognizing the Main Idea

What is the *main* idea or the *main point* of the article you have just read? Ask yourself, "What is the writer saying about the topic?" In a sentence or two, write the main idea of the article.

_____

_____

_____

Comprehension

True/False

Decide whether each statement is true or false according to the information in the article. Then put T (true) or F (false) in the blank to the left of the question number. Explain any "false" answers in the answer blanks that follow each question.

_____ 1. More Koreans emigrated to the United States in 1987 than in any other year.

_____

_____

_____ 2. Korea's growing economy makes apartments more affordable for the returning immigrants.

_____

_____

_____ 3. Because of its diverse society, Korea does not have a problem with racial conflict.

_____

_____

_____ 4. The reader can assume that the Korean immigrants who had successful businesses in the United States did not look forward to "starting over" in Korea.

_____

_____

_____ 5. A mom-and-pop store is a small business, usually owned and operated by members of a family.

_____

_____

_____ 6. After Koreans return to their native country, they cut all ties to the United States.

_____

_____

ANSWER THE FOLLOWING QUESTION IN YOUR OWN WORDS.

Why would a *glass ceiling* influence many Korean immigrants to become *entrepreneurs?*

Glossary

The numbers in front of the words indicate the paragraphs (in the reading) in which the words are found. Those items that are not numbered appear in the headings. Stressed syllables are underlined.

(3)	ailing (adj.)	sick
(5)	entrepreneur (n.)	a person who organizes and manages his or her own business
(5)	burgeoning (adj.)	growing
(5)	parlay (v.)	build on
(10)	drawback (n.)	disadvantage
	glass ceiling	a barrier to personal advancement, especially of women or members of ethnic minorities
(11)	shunt (v.)	put aside
(12)	franchise (n.)	a license granted by a company to an individual to market its product
(17)	saturate (v.)	overcrowd
(18)	break-even (adj.)	having equal gain and loss
	work ethic	the belief that work is morally good

The Decay of Families Is Global, Study Says

By TAMAR LEWIN

1   Around the world, in rich and poor countries alike, the structure of family life is undergoing profound changes, a new analysis of research from numerous countries has concluded.

2   "The idea that the family is a stable and cohesive unit in which father serves as economic provider and mother serves as emotional care giver is a myth," said Judith Bruce, an author of the study. "The reality is that trends like unwed motherhood, rising divorce rates, smaller households and the feminization of poverty are not unique to America, but are occurring worldwide."

3   The report, "Families in Focus," was issued today by the Population Council, an international nonprofit group based in New York that studies reproductive health. It analyzed a variety of existing demographic and household studies from dozens of countries worldwide.

4   These are among the major findings:
    Whether because of abandonment, separation, divorce or death of a spouse, marriages are dissolving with increasing frequency. In many developed countries, divorce rates doubled between 1970 and 1990, and in less developed countries, about a quarter of first marriages end by the time women are in their 40's.

5   Parents in their prime working years face growing burdens caring for children, who need to be supported through more years of education, and for their own parents, who are living longer into old age.

6   Unwed motherhood is increasingly common virtually everywhere, reaching as many as a third of all births in Northern Europe, for example.

7   Children in single-parent households—usually families with only a mother present—are much more likely to be poor than those who live with two parents, largely because of the loss of support from the absent fathers.

8   Even in households where fathers are present, mothers are carrying increasing economic responsibility for children.

9   The idea that families are changing in similar ways, even in very different cultures, should bring about new thinking on social policy, experts say, and in particular on the role government should play in supporting families.

10   "Most of the changes in the family that we think are home-grown are occurring everywhere," said Frank Furstenberg, a sociology professor at the University of Pennsylvania, a specialist in family demographics. "The mainspring of the worldwide change probably has to do with the economic status of women and changes in the gender-based division of labor."

11   Douglas Besharov, a resident scholar at the American Enterprise Institute, agrees that working women are the moving force behind many of the changes in the family.

12   "We are dealing here with the liberation of women," he said. "In the post-industrial age, when the earning power of men and women becomes quite equal, that creates a very different relationship between men and women and makes it easier for women to leave unhappy relationships."

13   The Population Council report says women tend to work longer hours than men, at home and on the job. In studies of 17 less developed countries, women's work hours exceeded men's by 30 percent. Data from 12 industrialized countries found that formally employed women worked about 20 percent longer hours than employed men.

14   Women's economic contributions also are becoming increasingly important. In Ghana, the report said, a third of households with children are maintained primarily by women. In the Philippines, women contribute about a third of households' cash income, but 55 percent of household support if the economic value of the women's activities at home, like gathering wood or growing food, is included.

15   In the United States, a Louis Harris survey released earlier this month found that nearly half of employed married women contribute half or more of their family's income.

16   "In most parts of the world, women have always been important providers," Ms. Bruce said. "But now," she added, "the form of their providing is more easily measurable, and more visible."

17   While the reason for entering the work force may vary from country to country, women everywhere are finding that to give their children an adequate life they must earn more money, she said.

18   "In traditional Bangladesh, it may be because the husband was much older, and died while the children were still young," she said. "In sub-Saharan Africa, a woman might have a baby premaritally and have no strong connection with the father, or she might have a husband who goes on to another polygamous marriage and supports the children of that union.

19   "In Asia the husband may have migrated for better economic opportunities and stopped sending money after a year or two. And everywhere, parents are finding that there are fewer jobs that pay enough to support a family."

20 Even among rural people in less developed countries, she said, the need for a cash income is becoming more pressing.

21 "Parents all over the world have an increasing awareness that their children will need literacy and numeracy," Ms. Bruce said. "That means that instead of having their 6-year-old working with them in the fields, they have to pay for school fees, uniforms, transportation and supplies. And while they can farm for food, they can't farm for school fees."

22 The fact that many developing countries have cut their spending on public education as part of their debt reduction plans creates further pressure on families, she said.

23 One apparent exception to the general trends is Japan, where single-parent households and unwed motherhood have remained relatively rare.

24 The Population Council report, written by Ms. Bruce, Cynthia B. Lloyd and Ann Leonard, found that while most countries have extensive data on women as mothers, there has been little research on men as fathers. But studies of parent-child interactions found no society in which fathers provided as much child care as mothers, and very few in which fathers had regular, close relationships with their young children.

25 And although fathers' income usually exceeds mothers' income, women usually contribute a larger proportion of their income to their household, while men keep more for their personal use.

26 Collecting child support is also difficult. The report says that among divorced fathers, three-quarters in Japan, almost two-thirds in Argentina, half in Malaysia and two-fifths in the United States do not pay child support.

27 The report emphasizes a need for new policies and programs to strengthen the father-child link—for example by allowing new fathers time off from their jobs, encouraging fathers to become involved in prenatal classes and familiarizing schoolage boys with the demands of child care.

28 "I think the conservative fear may be that all human beings are selfish at their core and that the pull of the market is so strong that women are going to become more like men, and invest less in their children," Professor Furstenberg said.

29 "But I think it's possible that we're moving into a world where men will behave more like women with regard to their children," he said. "The underlying question for the 21st century is how to create a system that allows all parents to invest in their children, both emotionally and financially."

DIVORCE RATES Divorces per 100 marriages

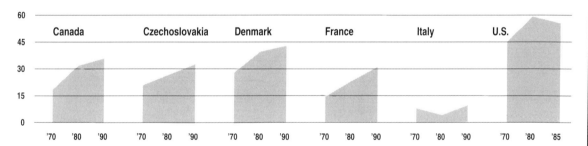

OUT-OF-WEDLOCK BIRTHS As a percentage of all births in each country or region

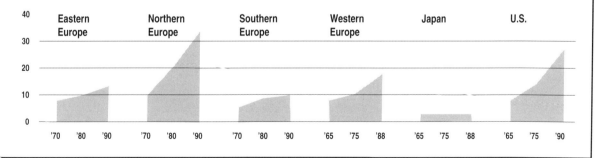

Comprehension

True/False

Decide whether each statement is true or false according to the information in the article. Then put T (true) or F (false) in the blank to the left of the question number. Explain any "false" answers in the answer blanks that follow each question.

_____ 1.   Dissimilar cultures are experiencing similar changes in the family.

_____

_____

_____ 2.   Unwed motherhood is chiefly responsible for the worldwide changes in the family.

_____

_____

_____ 3.   The reason that women everywhere are entering the workforce is to assert their independence.

_____

_____

_____ 4.   In the workplace women work fewer hours than men; in the home the opposite is true.

_____

_____

_____ 5.   The reader can **infer** that in the past, children of rural families in less developed countries had no formal schooling.

_____

_____

_____ 6. To become more involved in the care and upbringing of their children, fathers in the United States should model themselves after fathers in other societies.

_____

_____

_____ 7. Although employed women usually make less money than their husbands, the former contribute more money to the household.

_____

_____

Look at the Graph

_____ 8. The United States leads the way in divorces and out-of-wedlock births.

_____

_____

_____ 9. In the United States, the divorce rate increased steadily from 1970 to 1985.

_____

_____

_____10. Between 1970 and 1990, the divorce rate doubled in France.

_____

_____

_____11. Between 1970 and 1990, one-third of all births in northern Europe were to unwed mothers.

_____

_____

_____12. Japan has the least problem with illegitimacy.

_____

_____

EXPLAIN THE FOLLOWING EXCERPT FROM THE ARTICLE IN YOUR OWN WORDS.

"[The] fear may be that all human beings are selfish at their core and that the pull of the market is so strong that women are going to become more like men, and invest less in their children," . . . (par. 28)

Glossary

The numbers in front of the words indicate the paragraphs (in the reading) in which the words are found. Stressed syllables are underlined.

(2)	cohesive (adj.)	unified
(2)	myth (n.)	an unproved or false belief
(5)	prime (adj.)	most productive
(18)	polygamous (adj.)	having more than one spouse at the same time
(27)	prenatal classes	classes that teach soon-to-be parents how to care for a child